THE SHELL PILOT
TO THE SOUTH COAST HARBOURS

THE SHELL PILOT TO THE
SOUTH COAST HARBOURS

A Shell Guide

K. ADLARD COLES

author of
Creeks and Harbours of the Solent
Channel Harbours and Anchorages
North Brittany Harbours Pilot
North Biscay Pilot, With A. N. Black

with charts by
COLIN STEWART
Extra-Master, M.I.N.

FABER AND FABER

London

First published as Sailing on the South Coast
Reissued 1939 by Faber & Faber Ltd
3 Queen Square London WC1
Reprinted 1947 (twice)
Second edition with new title
Pocket Pilot for the South Coast 1950
Third edition 1962
Fourth completely new and revised edition 1968
with present title, reprinted 1971
Interim new edition 1973, with correction pages

It is regretted that neither author nor publisher can
accept responsbility for errors or omissions

Printed in Great Britain by
W & J Mackay Limited, Chatham

ISBN 0 571 04828 5

ACKNOWLEDGEMENTS

In the first edition of this book I was indebted to Mr. T. L. Stocken for his collaboration, to Commander W. B. Luard, R.N.Rtd., for information on the West Country ports and to Messrs. Imray, Laurie, Norie & Wilson for their permission to take extracts from *The Pilot's Guide to the English Channel*. For the revised 1962 edition I added my thanks to Captain C. Stewart, Extra Master, and Mrs. Stewart for their work on the harbour plans and for the chapters on the Scilly Isles and Rye and to Mr. J. Kentish for revision east of Lyme Regis.

In this new edition for 1968 I repeat my acknowledgement to the foregoing. Captain and Mrs. Stewart have revised the charts and Mr. J. Kentish has rechecked the Solent ports. In addition I am grateful to Mr. John Patterson for corrections from Ramsgate to Rye, Mr. Michael Gilkes for Newhaven and Shoreham, Mr. G. J. Dunster and the Harbour Master for Chichester, the honorary secretary of the Lock's Sailing Club for Langston and Mr. D. Ide for harbours west of the Solent, other than those which I have checked myself. I would also like to thank all the Harbour Masters who have been most co-operative.

I am indebted to the Controller of H.M. Stationery Office and the Hydrographer of the Navy for permission to base the plans on Admiralty charts. Tidal constants and rise of tide are supplied by the Liverpool Observatory and Tidal Institute with the permission of H.M. Stationery Office. Times of tidal streams and some particulars of Shoreham Harbour have been taken from the *Channel Pilot, Vol. I*, also by permission of H.M. Stationery Office. The aerial photographs have been acknowledged under the individual pictures. The brief lists of the launching sites are based on information from harbour masters, personal observation and the booklet: *Getting Afloat: Light Craft Launching Sites*. I recommend this publication to yachtsmen who make a practice of towing their boats and want to know all the launching sites in Great Britain and Ireland. It can be obtained from Link House, Dingwall Avenue, Croydon, CR9 2TA.

THE SHELL PILOT at Sea

Paper is notoriously liable to suffer damage from
damp and to help in preserving your copy while
at sea we recommend you should obtain the
plastic sleeve with special closure
designed to protect the book when it is lying
open or closed. Please send 6 new pence to

Shell-Mex and B.P. Ltd.,
Advertising Services Division (Publications)
Strand, London W.C.2,

and ask for a sleeve to be sent to you.

CONTENTS

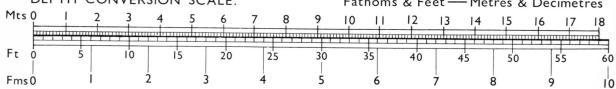

DEPTH CONVERSION SCALE.   Fathoms & Feet —— Metres & Decimetres

FOREWORD

In the 1968 edition of *The Shell Pilot to the South Coast Harbours* no major change has been made in the general arrangement of the book, which provides a concise work of reference for owners of yachts up to 6 ft. draft. It consists as before of three parts: harbours and anchorages, passage notes and harbour plans.

Many alterations have been made on the harbour plans to conform with the latest Admiralty charts, but the datum remains the same at approximately M.L.W.S. until the next edition, by which time it is anticipated all the Admiralty charts will have been converted to L.A.T. datum and the harbour plans may be redrawn accordingly. The new datum is explained on pages 13 and 223.

It is emphasized again that the plans in this book are intended to be associated with up-to-date *Nautical Almanac* and coastal charts. They provide concise information leading to the principal harbours and estuaries, but for navigation in the upper reaches, such as at Falmouth, Plymouth or Salcombe, large scale charts are recommended, as they show detail which cannot be reproduced on small scale. Likewise, it is not possible within the compass of a pocket pilot book to give all the navigational information and other details available in the official publications, as for example local bye-laws. Such regulations exist in most commercial harbours. They may include speed limits, usually of 5 to 6 knots, and sometimes provide that small, shallow draft vessels must keep out of the way of ships confined to narrow fairways because of their draft. This is only common sense, and likewise it is important that visiting yachtsmen should know and obey the regulating signals for entry into commercial harbours. Harbour dues are not listed as they are liable to alteration, upwards but never downwards. *The Pilot's Guide to the English Channel*, published by Imray, Laurie, Norie & Wilson, Wych House, St. Ives, Hunts, is recommended to those who desire a more comprehensive work. My own books, *Creeks and Harbours of the Solent* and *Channel Harbours and Anchorages* (Solent to Portland—Barfleur to St. Malo including the Channel Islands) also cover parts of the coast in greater detail with larger charts and photographs.

Great care has been taken in the compilation and revision of this book, but the reader should recognize the possibility of error which occurs in individual work without the aid of independent checking, and that no responsbility can be accepted for mistakes or omissions. Changes in sand formations and bars and of lights, buoys and beacons are frequent, and this fact should be recognized when approaching a strange harbour, especially if a considerable time has elapsed since the date of publication. It is not possible to issue amendment sheets of this book and the reader is recommended to refer to the weekly Admiralty 'Notices to Mariners' or to Norie's Bulletin of Alterations and Corrections for 'Y' and 'C' charts. They are obtainable from Imray, Laurie, Norie & Wilson Limited, together with a series of large-scale 'Y' and 'C' charts of the coast and estuaries.

A Note on the Amendments (*Interim New Edition 1973*)

This interim new edition of *The Shell Pilot to the South Coast Harbours* is issued to meet the requirements of yachtsmen in the transition period pending the completion of the new issue Admiralty charts for the whole of the South Coast of England, with depths and drying areas reduced to the datums of L.A.T. and expressed in metres.

Not until then will it be sensible to start the preparation of a new edition to conform with these fundamental changes. As the work will involve new drawings of the 60 harbour plans, a complete revision of the text and possibly the resetting of the whole of the type in the book before printing, a considerable time must elapse before a completely revised edition can be available to the public.

In the meantime this interim new edition has been brought up to date by means of amendments and corrections which appear on pages 218 to 224. These are listed harbour by harbour and are followed by an explanation and tables so that the existing harbour plans in the book may easily be reconciled wth the new issue Admiralty charts in course of publication and the Tide Tables. The lists of Coastguard, Life-Boat Stations and Radio Beacons have been omitted as this information is readily available in *Reed's Nautical Almanac.*

Alterations in this edition include a number of new or changed lights and the principal improvements, including new marinas, which I have observed when cruising to all the harbours, including those in the Solent, between Chichester and Portland. I also visited most—but not all—of the principal ports in the West Country and the Isles of Scilly, where I found few changes. I have also checked the harbour plans with the latest charts available and Light List Vol. A and listed the alterations. The harbours from Ramsgate to Littlehampton have been visited for me by two experienced cruising friends, to whom I am most grateful for their work.

K.A.C.
January, 1973

EXPLANATION OF TERMS AND NOTATION OF CHARTS

High Water The constants used are supplied by the Liverpool Observatory and Tidal Institute giving the mean difference in reference to Dover. Simply turn up in the *Nautical Almanac* or *Yachting World Diary* the time of H.W. at Dover, and add or subtract the constant given for the particular harbour. These constants are only approximate in respect of the harbours situated at a long distance from Dover; for greater accuracy refer to time of H.W. and constants of local standard ports which are given in Reed's *Nautical Almanac*. Rise is given for each port at M.H.W.S. and M.H.W.N. above chart datum, but approximations are given where data are not available.

In the Solent there are double or long durations of high water. Constants are given for the mean differences on Dover. At spring tides the first high water is earlier than at neaps and this characteristic is even more evident at Christchurch and Poole.

Charted Depths and Datums. The charted depths given in this book indicate the depth of water *below chart datum*, or the drying heights (figures *underlined*) above it. The figures for the rise of tide indicate heights above chart datums, which in this book conform with the datums used in the appropriate British Admiralty Charts up to 1965. These may be taken as approximately the level of mean low water springs, abbreviated to M.L.W.S.

In 1965, the Admiralty commenced adjusting datums for British charts in accordance with the International Agreement and modern practice. The new datums represent for each locality the level of the lowest astro-

The datums of the harbour plans in this interim new edition remain as before. For reconcilation of their datums, which are approximately M.L.W.S., with the L.A.T. datums of the new issue charts and Tide Tables (and for a conversion scale in fathoms, feet and metres) see pages 218 to 224.

Approach The directions assume that the vessel is approaching from seaward, and objects are described on the port or starboard hand of a ship entering the harbour.

Notation of Charts—Lights. Lights outside harbours only are shown, except (1) leading lights placed inside, and (2) important buoys used for proceeding up harbour.

Lights are symbolized, word 'light' or 'Lt.' omitted.

Nature of light is noted, e.g. F., fixed, Gp. Fl., group flashing, etc., and in the case of other than white lights, the colour, e.g. R., G., etc. Periodicity, where given, is that of 1967 corrected where necessary on pages 218 to 222. Even so, lights are liable to alteration, and reference should be made to the latest light list or almanac. Combination lights are noted, e.g. W.R.G., etc., but sequence of coloured arcs does not necessarily correspond to order of notation. An arc with a dashed line indicates a white sector, double dashes a green sector and a continuous line a red sector.

Buoys are symbolized, word 'buoy' omitted. Colour and shape are not described, but symbol conforms to shape of buoy, and where scale allows, to configuration, i.e. solid black for black buoys, outline or patched shading only for white or red, chequers and stripes shown as such.

Beacons are either symbolized or shown as small round 'O'. Point where pole crosses base line indicates exact position. Topographical details marked on shore, e.g. coast-guard, tower, house, etc., are in exact position and will give true bearing. Centre of object in each case.

Coloured Area, heavy stipple, indicates parts which dry out at low water. Blue indicates parts where there are less than 6 ft. at M.L.W.S., and is bounded by dotted line. All over 1 fathom is left white.

Anchorage Symbol (⚓) is intended to draw attention to proximity of anchorage, and does not necessarily indicate precise or only spot for letting go.

Minor posts, withys, dolphins, etc., inside harbours are sometimes precluded by scale.

Abbreviations Where these are used in the text they are the recognized standard abbreviations:

H.W.	High water
L.W.	Low water
L.A.T.	Lowest astronomical tide
M.H.W.S.	Mean high water springs
M.H.W.N.	Mean high water neaps
M.L.W.S.	Mean low water springs
M.L.W.N.	Mean low water neaps
Occ.	Occulting
Qk.	Quick
Ro. Bn.	Radio beacon
Tr.	Tower
Bn.	Beacon
cheq.	Chequered
ev.	Every
F.	Fixed
Fl.	Flashing
Gp.	Group
Iso.	Isophase
Rev.	Revolving
E.F. Horn	Electric fog horn
Dia.	Diaphone
Nauto.	Nautophone
Tyfon	Compressed air horn
Mag.	Magnetic
m.	Metres
M.	Miles (visible)
B.	Black
B.W.	Black and white
G.	Green
H.	Horizontal
Or.	Orange
R.	Red
R.W.	Red and white
S.	Stripes
Sph.	Spherical
V.	Vertical
W.	White

For complete list see the Admiralty explanation of symbols and abbreviations, Chart No. 5011.

RAMSGATE

Plan No. 1

High Water + 0 h. 20 m. Dover.
Rise 16.2 ft. springs; 13.0 ft. neaps.
Depths 6 ft. just outside entrance deepening between the pier ends to 10 ft. and then shoaling inside towards the shore. The depths off the entrance are variable and the amount of water in the harbour is considerably influenced by the direction of the wind. Alongside west pier there is normally 7 ft. and east pier 10 ft. M.L.W.S. Water in the inner harbour is impounded by gates and maintained at about 10 to 15 ft. and is non-tidal. Commercial traffic uses the western end of the inner basin and yachts are moored at the eastern pontoons.

1. *Ramsgate Harbour from cliffs looking east.*

RAMSGATE is the most easterly of the harbours south of the Thames. It is conveniently situated for yachts making passage from the Channel to the North Sea or vice versa. The town is adjacent to the harbour and all facilities are available.

Approach and Entrance Approaching from the south either the Ramsgate channel or the Gull Stream can be used. The Ramsgate channel lies between Sandwich flats on the west and the Brake sand on the east. It is buoyed and after passing through the channel the North Fairway buoy (red can) will be identified and left to port. Then steer for the entrance on a line from North Fairway buoy to a white diamond mark on the east pier below the watch-house. On the flood the tide sets strongly east across the entrance and allowance must be made to prevent being swept against the east pierhead. Approaching from the Gull Stream steer to northward until the breakwaters bear 290° and enter by the Old Cudd channel, referred to below.

From the eastward or northward use the Old Cudd channel in least depth 7 ft. This is entered by bringing the light pillar on the east pierhead in line with the lighthouse on the west pierhead at 290°. This leaves the Quern red can buoy (at the north end of the Quern shoal) close to port and close to starboard the unmarked spit of the Dike sand.

When about ½ cable from the east pierhead bear away to the south giving the east pierhead a wide berth of ½ cable and enter the harbour on the leading line from south. This will avoid the strong tidal set close to the pier and also the shoal off it. Note that the shoals outside the harbour are constantly shifting and the buoys and marks are moved from time to time.

The lock gates to the inner harbour open about 2 hrs. before H.W. and close at H.W. Berthing directions are given from the watch-house on the east pier.

Tidal Signals A black ball displayed close up on flagstaff on Sion Hill over inner harbour indicates depth of 10 ft. or over between pierheads; at half mast indicates less than 10 ft. At night the tidal light on West pier is red fixed when depth is 10 ft. or over; green when less than 10 ft. During fog a bell at East pier 10 strokes every quarter hour indicates 10 ft. or over; 5 strokes slowly less than 10 ft.

Traffic Signals from East pier flagstaff: black flag and bell rung quickly (at night bell only) indicates vessel(s) about to enter harbour and outward vessels to keep clear. Two black flags (red fixed light night) vessels may not enter or approach harbour.

Lights East pierhead Lt. Occ. ev. 10 sec. 4 M. This is also front light for north and east leading line, the rear light is west pier F.R. or G. (see tide signal) 7 M. and these lights in line are 290°.

West pier is front light F.R. or G. for south leading line and in line with F.G. light 4 M. high up on east cliff. These in line bear 021°: *Fog Signal* Bell from east pier.

2. *Ramsgate entrance approaching from south approx. on leading line 021°. This is the only correct angle of approach.*

3. *Ramsgate entrance from south-east. It is from this angle of approach that a sailing yacht would risk being set on to the east pier.*

4. *Ramsgate, west pier and light looking into harbour and gate to inner harbour.*

5. *Ramsgate, outer harbour yacht moorings to port of entrance.*

Anchorage Outside, south of harbour in Pegwell Bay under favourable conditions. No anchoring is permitted in the harbour as the central channel must be kept clear for larger vessels and the remainder is foul with moorings. Hovercraft kept in N.E. corner.

Visiting yachts are usually directed from the watch-house to lie by the wall of the west pier in 8 to 10 ft. Berthing directions for the inner harbour are given by the gate-keeper as the yacht enters. Generally yachts berth on pontoons at the east end. The level is maintained at about 10 to 15 ft.

Facilities Water at all piers on application. Petrol and oil, etc. available. Shops adjacent. Early closing Thursday. Boatbuilders and repairers. Patent slip and scrubbing. Launching site slipways in inner and outer harbour—see Harbour Master. Yacht club: R. Temple Y.C.

6. *Ramsgate, facing north-east across the inner harbour. Yachts berth at pontoons in the eastern part.*

SANDWICH

Plan No. 2

High Water + o h. 15 m. Dover.

Tides *The ebb runs for 9 hrs. and the flood for 3 hrs. at Sandwich Town, but the current continues upstream for a short time after H.W. and downstream for a short time after L.W.*

Depths *Entrance channel and river shallow. At H.W. springs navigable with a maximum draft of 10 ft. or 6½ ft. at neaps as far as Sandwich.*

SANDWICH, one of the Cinque Ports, lies 4½ miles from the mouth of the River Stour. It is an historically interesting town. Visiting yachts lying by the town quay are within 2 min. walk of the town centre and there is a good hotel adjacent to the quay. Coasters sometimes use the quay to unload timber and ballast.

Approaches and Entrance The entrance to the River Stour lies at the south-west corner of Pegwell Bay about ¾ mile south-west of Ramsgate. Pegwell Bay dries out except for a narrow gulley carrying the river water. The channel across the bay is well marked with buoys, red and white to port and black to starboard. These buoys are moved from time to time to allow for shifting sands. Approach only in good weather.

7. *Sandwich. River Stour just inside entrance looking upstream, showing conspicuous old water tower and new power station in building which will be prominent.*

19

From North Fairway buoy which lies $3\frac{1}{2}$ cables south-west of Ramsgate east breakwater light, steer 266° true for $6\frac{1}{2}$ cables to the outer buoy, then follow the channel. Once inside the river keep to the middle. There is a dubious 10 ft. M.H.W.S. and $6\frac{1}{2}$ ft. M.H.W.N. as far as Sandwich, with sludge bottom. The swing bridge above the quay may be opened by giving 1 hour's notice; there is then 12 miles of navigable water for yachts and boats up to 4 ft. draft and a rail bridge with about 12 ft. clearance. *Warning* Just inside the river near the water tank on the starboard hand is a dolphin which covers at H.W. There is only a small pole topmark showing. Leave to starboard.

Lights There are no lights or fog signals. Do not attempt to enter at night or in fog without local knowledge.

Anchorage and Quay Under favourable conditions anchor 2 or 3 cables west of North Fairway buoy whilst waiting for the tide to enter. Once inside the river there is no anchorage or landing place until Sandwich Town quay. Richborough wharf is private. At Sandwich the bottom is mud over chalk. For deep draft yachts it is wise to make preparations for drying out by the wall as the layer of mud is not very deep.

Facilities Water at Town quay on application to Borough Surveyor. Petrol at garage near quay. Shops. Early closing Wednesday. Hotels. Yacht yard and chandlery just above bridge, slip 40 ft. × 5–6 ft. draft.

8. *Sandwich. River Stour near mouth, looking upstream towards Richborough wharf.*

9. *Sandwich—quay and swing bridge. Bell Hotel on left and yacht yard above bridge.*

DOVER

Plan No. 3

Rise of Tide 19.1 *ft. springs;* 15.1 *ft. neaps; but irregular, depending on wind conditions.*

Depths *Dover is a large artificial harbour, divided into two parts. The big expanse of the outer harbour is a deep water port. The smaller western part between the Admiralty pier and the Prince of Wales pier has from 2 fathoms to 5 fathoms in the entrance, but the depths gradually reduce towards the inner tidal harbour,* which dries out at L.W. except for a narrow channel a foot or two deep. Beyond this are the inner basins. The Wellington dock, which is used by yachts, has 22½ ft. springs, 16 ft. neaps. The eastern dock is deep.*

DOVER is a busy commercial port and its harbour is also considerably used by yachts, owing to its convenient position at the south-east corner of England. In recent years yachting has very much come to the fore. The town is a pleasant one and all facilities are available.

Approach and Entrance Dover harbour is some 2 miles south-west of the South Foreland, and by day the long breakwaters make the harbour easy to identify,

10. *Dover—panorama facing eastwards from cliffs.*

11. *Dover—outer harbour from Prince of Wales pier looking across yacht anchorage to castle.*

12. *Dover—looking into inner tidal harbour with Granville dock in background. Yachts pass up this harbour and turn to starboard at end for Wellington dock.*

and at night its numerous powerful lights are unmistakable.

Yachts are not permitted to use the western entrance, but enter by the eastern one. Entrance should preferably be made between 2 hrs. before to 1 hr. after high water in order to avoid the strength of the tidal streams and eddies around the mole-heads, where it is often rough. A look out should be kept for the entry signals, which are as follows.

Entrance Signals Outer harbour, east entrance exhibited from mast.

By Day—Three red balls in triangle: vessels are permitted to leave and no vessel is to enter or approach so as to obstruct the entrance. Two red balls vertical: vessels may enter with permission and no vessel is to leave or approach so as to obstruct the entrance. Permission to enter must in each case be obtained from the signal station. Three red balls vertical: entrance is closed, for entering or leaving.

At Night—One orange light at north end of detached breakwater and two green lights vertical at seaward end of eastern arm. These lights *when shown seaward* and obscured towards the harbour indicate that vessels may enter with permission and unless these lights are being shown seaward no vessel is to enter or approach to obstruct the passage of any outward-bound vessel. Permission to enter must in each case be obtained from the signal station. These lights *when shown towards the harbour and obscured seaward* indicate that vessels are permitted to leave and unless these lights are being shown towards the harbour no vessel is to leave or approach to obstruct the passage of any inward-bound vessel. Three red lights vertical: entrance closed for entering or leaving.

Inner Harbour When approaching the inner harbour leading to the basins avoid the Mole Head rocks on the north wide of fairway extending south-westwards off the end of the north pier. Anchorage is not permitted between Admiralty and Prince of Wales piers. While waiting the tide yachts should anchor in the outer harbour or, with sufficient rise, make fast on the port hand harbour wall outside the Wellington dock until the lock gates open.

Signals From mast at south pier or by night at north and south pierheads: red flag indicates vessels permitted to pass inwards. No signal indicates vessels permitted to pass outwards. Red lights shown seaward indicate vessels permitted to pass inward. Red lights shown shoreward indicate vessels may pass outwards. *Inner Dock Signals* from mast at Granville dock head for both docks: blue and white pennant or 2 white lights vertical: entry permitted. One black ball or two red lights vertical: vessel leaving, entry not permitted.

Anchorage, etc. (1) East of and protected from west by the Prince of Wales pier, as near to the shore as soundings permit. Anchorage is prohibited outside a line joining the south end of Prince of Wales pier to the south end of the Eastern Arm, and within the whole of the Inner Harbour. (2) Harbour Board moorings off Yacht Club. The club also has moorings, but permission to use one must first be obtained from the club. (3) Yachts are no longer permitted to use the former submarine basin, now known as the Eastern Dock. (4) In bad weather pass into inner Wellington dock, which is opened 1½ hrs. before high water and closes H.W. Visiting yachts are allowed to stay for a period depending upon what berths are available. The Granville Dock is not available to yachts.

Lights At western entrance light Fl. ev. 7½ sec. 14 M. is exhibited from a white tower on the Admiralty pier on the west side. On the detached mole knuckle there is a light occ. white seaward, red shoreward, 10 sec. 12 M. Green fixed light at end of Prince of Wales pier vis. 4 M. At the eastern entrance two fixed green lights or three fixed red (see entrance signals). There are lights at the eastern dock and elsewhere—see chart. Alterations possible when western entrance is re-opened.

Fog Signals Diaphone (2) ev. 30 sec. at south end of east pier. Bell (2) ev. 15 sec. at Prince of Wales pier. Siren (2) 10 sec. at Camber west pier when required by ferries. Diaphone (3) at end of Admiralty pier.

Facilities Water at Prince of Wales pier and docks. All yacht chandlery, petrol, oil and stores available. Early closing day, Wednesday. Scrubbing at slipway, Wellington dock. Yacht yards. Yacht club: R. Cinque Ports Y.C. Launching site: from centre of promenade up to 16 ft. Car park. Two stations. Buses to all parts.

13. *Dover—entrance to Wellington dock with gates open. Lie by wall on port hand whilst waiting for gates to open.*

14. *Dover—Granville dock and beyond the Wellington dock in which yachts are berthed.* [Photo: Aero Films]

FOLKESTONE

Plan No. 4

High Water —0 h. 12 m. Dover.
Rise 20.6 ft. springs; 16.4 ft. neaps.
Depths *The outer harbour is dredged to a least depth of 17 ft. and is formed by the breakwater which extends into deep water. In the entrance to the inner harbour there is 18 ft. at M.H.W.S. and from 11 to 14 ft. M.H.W.S. within the harbour, and at neaps 3 ft. less. At L.W. it dries out.*

FOLKESTONE HARBOUR is only suitable for yachts with legs or those prepared to dry out by the rough wall at the east pier. It is not a good refuge in bad weather. The harbour faces east but the entrance itself receives extra protection from the west by a long breakwater built for the B.R. steamers and which forms the outer harbour. The inner harbour is mostly used by fishing boats which are equipped with legs. The town itself has all the facilities of a summer holiday resort.

Approach and Entrance Folkestone is about $5\frac{1}{2}$ miles westward of Dover and is the only large town situated on the coast between Dungeness and the Foreland. The town is thus easy to recognize and the

15. *Folkestone. The harbour and town from east.*

harbour lies nearer the eastern end of the town, behind a conspicuous outer breakwater. There are rocky ledges to the west of the breakwater and east of the harbour entrance. Of these the Mole Head rocks, less than 2 cables east of the inner end of the outer breakwater, and the ledges off Copt Point are the more dangerous. To clear these when approaching from the east keep the South Foreland well open of the Dover cliffs. By night, the South Foreland light is masked northward of 58° true, so that the vessel should not go northward of the arc of the light. Eddy on E. stream.

Tidal Signals are not given for yachts, but only for steamers. There is plenty of water 3 hrs. either side of H.W. for yachts. Yachts should exercise caution when the following signals are flying. Black flag on end of outer breakwater means steamer leaving port. One, two or three balls means mail boat entering. From south pier, red flag or red light means steamer entering inner harbour. Yachts inside wait to leave.

Lights etc. Outer breakwater light, white Gp. Fl. (2) ev. 10 sec., vis. 12 M., height 45 ft. Fog. Diaphone (4) for steamers only.

Inner harbour—south pierhead. Gong occasional for steamers only. Ht. 60 ft. East pierhead Qk. Fl.

Anchorage (1) Outside off the breakwater head, clear of steamers' fairway. Exposed and the holding ground indifferent. (2) Inside east pier on legs or alongside east pier, bottom sand, dry for about 3 hrs.

The swing bridge at west end of harbour is now fixed, so that the western end can be used only by boats able to pass under the bridge.

Facilities Water at quay. Petrol at Quayside. Good shopping centre, early closing Wednesday. Station, and buses to all parts. Yacht club: Folkestone S.C.

16.   *Folkestone. Inner harbour looking across entrance which is on right. Firm clean bottom to dry on legs or lie by wall*

17.   *Folkestone. Inner harbour looking along south pier and old swing bridge which is now fixed. Small boat harbour beyond.*

RYE

Plan No. 5

High Water *at bar* —o *h.* 05 *m. Dover.*

Rise *in bay* 23.1 *ft. springs;* 18.3 *ft. neaps. Rise at entrance* 19 *ft. and less further up.*

Depths *Bar practically dries out M.L.W.S. In the channel there is only a fresh water trickle about 2 ft. deep or less. At high water springs there is* 11 *to* 15 *ft. in the harbour alongside the catwalk staging and* 5½ *to* 9½ *ft. at neaps.*

Rye harbour is ¾ mile within the entrance, and is a small village. The town itself is another 2 miles up the river, which is navigable at high water and is occasionally used by a few small trading ships; it is one of the Cinque ports and so charming that it attracts many visitors—there are good hotels.

Rye harbour entrance had a somewhat bad reputation owing to the loss of the lifeboat crew west of the entrance in 1928. Since then, however, the entrance has been improved and it is clearly marked. Given an offshore wind and fair weather and the right state of tide strangers should not find the entrance unduly difficult. A south-west wind Force 4 is definitely uncomfortable and probably too much for a first attempt. Power is desirable, as the tide runs very hard

18.　*The entrance to Rye from the south-east (at L.W.). The leading marks on Admiralty chart (churches in line) are not conspicuous from a small boat. However, the west pier is prominent.*

19.　*The entrance and east pier at H.W.S. from the root of the west pier. The port hand cages mark the submerged training wall.*

in the narrow channel—the flood is stronger than the ebb, which is unusual in rivers.

Approach and Entrance The entrance lies at the apex of Rye Bay. From the eastward follow the low coast from Dungeness for some 7 miles keeping about a mile offshore until the conspicuous west pier and the tripod beacon are seen. Westwards of the entrance the shore is also low (but hills behind) for a distance of 5 miles to Fairlight, which is high and can be recognized by the square tower of the church, and its coastguard station.

The entrance and channel to Rye harbour, which is from 100 to 150 ft. wide, lies between the east pier and the west pier from which extends a long training wall to sea and inland of the entrance. This training wall is covered at high water. It is marked by a series of poles with cage topmarks but there is a considerable length unmarked to seaward (which is lower), at its extremity there stands a tripod pile beacon 22 ft. high. The east pier is also long, though it does not extend as far seaward and at the end of it there is a light post. At M.H.W.S. springs the tops of this pier (or groyne) are just showing but it is marked by two posts with conical topmarks.

The bar varies in position but around H.W. this is of little consequence. If the 'sea' permits, an approach from the south-east is perhaps to be preferred but if approaching from south-west give west beacon a wide berth and open up entrance. Within the entrance a course mid-channel or to the east of it is quite safe, although the deeper water is on the west side. However, care must be taken on the flood that in draughts over the training wall, which is of varying height, do not effect steering. The cage beacons are mostly fixed to the inside edge of the training wall.

The entrance must not even be approached at L.W. The best time to enter is from 1 hr. before H.W. and the best time to leave is not later than 1 hr. after H.W. (but for yachts of moderate draft $2\frac{1}{2}$ hrs. either side is possible with care at springs). On the east side of the harbour, about $\frac{3}{4}$ mile within the entrance, tidal signals are shown.

Tide Signals $\frac{3}{4}$ mile inland east of Rye harbour
Day (on yard arm)—7 ft. on bar, red flag (not often displayed); 8 ft. on bar, one ball on yard; 9 ft. on bar, one ball on *each* yard; 10 ft. on bar, one ball at masthead only; 11 ft. on bar, one ball at masthead, one ball on yard; 12 ft on bar, one ball at masthead, one ball *on each yard*.

Night (automatic from small lighthouse)—7–10 ft. on bar, a green light; over 10 ft. a red light.

Lights From beacon on western groyne extension, red light, Fl. ev. 5 sec. vis. 6 M.; on eastern pier end, light, Fl. ev. $2\frac{1}{2}$ sec., vis. 4 M. and two Qk. Fl. G. lights on the east side of the channel—these are in line 329°. Tide signal lights are also exhibited as stated above.

20.   *Looking up river from the slip at Rye harbour (near H.W.). Yachts on right are at the catwalk staging.*

21. *The entrance taken from west pier facing northward.*

Anchorage Yachts usually bring up at Rye harbour about a mile from entrance and about 2 miles from Rye town. Yachts moor on east side alongside stagings provided for the purpose where they will lie afloat for about 4 hrs. and take the bottom which is hard muddy shingle. The large range of tide calls for careful mooring, and winds blowing on to the staging have been the cause of many broken masts or damaged spreaders. The actual footway on the catwalk is submerged by a foot or so at H.W.S., although the tops of the staging and handrails are still above water. A vacant berth may indicate wreckage below water—always consult Harbour Master.

Facilities Water is available from a hose pipe at the south end of catwalk staging—apply to Harbour

22. *Looking downstream at L.W.S., catwalk staging on left. (Note Harbour Master's house and Tide Sig. lighthouse centre distance.)*

Master (Tel. Camber 225). Petrol and oil at Strand quay. Stores at Rye town 2 miles away, or limited supply in Rye harbour or at caravan site to south of village by the Martello tower. Early closing day, Tuesday. P.O. at harbour and town. Small boat-builders. Launching site: slip with road access at Rye harbour village, but is only usable for a few hours either side of H.W. (a power cable marked by beacons runs across near here to the lighthouse). Yacht club: Rye Harbour S.C. Station at Rye town. Bus service from harbour to town, whence buses to all parts.

NEWHAVEN

Plan No. 6

High Water —o h. 13 m. Dover.
Rise 20.7 *ft. springs;* 15.9 *ft. neaps.*
Depths 12 *to* 14 *ft. M.L.W.S. in the entrance; from* 8 *to* 12 *ft. along east wharf to Sleeper's Hole, and not less than* 7 *ft. above this up to the bridge. Silting and dredging continually occurring.*

NEWHAVEN is the best harbour between Portsmouth and Dover. The town itself is not interesting, but the distance by bus to Seaford or Eastbourne is short, and there are pleasant walks if weather-bound.

There is a regular steamer service to Dieppe and the harbour is used by other commercial vessels. The cross-Channel boats warp off by means of a steel hawser run across the harbour and also incoming ones swing by this method.

23. *Newhaven breakwater and view across bay to Seaford Head.*

24. *Newhaven entrance from end of breakwater.*

Approach and Entrance Newhaven harbour lies just over 7 miles west of Beachy Head (see Passage Notes), and 3 miles west of Seaford Head. The town of Seaford is 5 miles westward of Beachy Head and for some 2 miles west of Seaford the shore is low and shingly. At the western end of Seaford Bay is Burrow Head, and just eastward at the foot of this is Newhaven. The big breakwater at the entrance is conspicuous and makes an easily recognizable landmark.

From the eastward stand well away from Seaford Head and steer for position off Burrow Head. Alter course when the entrance bears north, and leave to the westward the outer breakwater, steering in toward the eastern pier, which is some 3 cables away. In bad weather, with an onshore wind, there is an awkward sea off the entrance southward of the breakwater. Steer up mid-channel observing signals shown at southern end of west pier. Within $\frac{1}{2}$ mile of shore, the west-going stream starts about $1\frac{1}{2}$ to 2 hrs. before H.W.

Signals By day signals consist of black spherical shapes (or balls) displayed from mast at base of lighthouse on West Pier. One black ball indicates a vessel may enter but not leave. Two black balls vertical that a vessel may not enter but may leave. Three black balls,

32

25.   *Newhaven harbour, showing marina on west side. [Photo: Aero Films]*

port temporarily closed to all traffic. By night from lighthouse. Green all round indicates that a vessel may enter but not leave. Red light, may leave but not enter.

Three red vertical, port temporarily closed.

Lights etc. At end of outer (western) breakwater light Gp. occ. (2) ev. 10 sec. vis. 12 M.; at end of eastern pier, isophase green light 5 sec. Small F. red light on west pier and F. green on east pier, a cable inside entrance. Diaphone outer breakwater head ev. 30 sec. Tide gauge near base of lighthouse on west pier.

Anchorage and Berths (1) Outside off Seaford in settled weather, dangerous if wind shifts onshore. (2) All yachts should seek instructions from Harbour Watch House on west side of harbour. Space is limited but limited duration mooring sometimes available at berths on east side of harbour, with 9 ft. M.L.W.S. (3) Some berthing facilities available in marina in Sleeper's Hole, 3 cables within entrance on porthand side. Marina Watch House at head of southern Marina jetty.

Facilities Petrol, oil and water from marina fuelling pontoon. Ship chandlers, and all stores obtainable. Early closing day, Wednesday. Yacht yard, yacht marina, gridirons and scrubbing hard. Launching site at Sleeper's Hole on application at Cresta Marine, also opposite Cantell's chandlery on application at shop. Yacht Club: Newhaven & Seaford S.C. Station and numerous buses to all parts.

SHOREHAM

Standard Port —0 *h.* 03 *m. Dover.*
Rise 18.1 *ft. springs;* 13.6 *ft. neaps.*
Depths 7 *ft. on leading line outside entrance, but subject to shoaling. Inside dredged to* 8½ *ft. to Prince Philip Lock, or* 5½ *ft. to Prince George Lock. Water level in canal 23 ft. as far as the turning basin. The western channel, which is the old river bed, is dredged to depths shown on Plan No. 8. Dredged depths are liable to silting and only hold good immediately after dredging.*

SHOREHAM HARBOUR consists of a western channel which is the mouth of the River Adur, and a short eastern arm leading through lock gates to the Southwick canal.

Superficially Shoreham is a good yachting harbour, as once through the locks into Southwick canal there is complete shelter and all facilities, besides being in easy reach of London. However, Shoreham is increasingly a commercial port with little room for private vessels. It is not possible here to summarize the 26 pages of Byelaws which are obtainable from the Harbour Master.

Approach and Entrance Shoreham harbour en-

26. *Shoreham. Looking north-east from just outside the entrance, showing end of breakwater and the two conspicuous power stations.* [*Photo: Cdr. Erroll Bruce*]

trance is about $3\frac{1}{2}$ miles west of Brighton West Pier. The most conspicuous landmarks are the twin chimneys of the power station about $\frac{3}{4}$ mile ENE of the entrance (marked by red lights), and another pair about $3\frac{3}{4}$ cables eastward of them. The entrance itself lies between two conspicuous concrete breakwaters.

The shallowing water in the approach and at the entrance can be very rough in strong winds if at all onshore, particularly on the ebb tide. Newhaven is a better port of refuge.

From the westward avoid Church rocks (least depth 3 ft.), about $1\frac{1}{2}$ miles west of the entrance, and over $\frac{1}{4}$ mile offshore. About $1\frac{1}{4}$ miles eastward of the entrance there are the Jenny ground rocks (least depth 5 ft.) about 3 cables offshore. A conical B.Y. vert. striped buoy about 3 cables ESE of the entrance marks the outer end of a sewer outfall. An obstruction is charted approximately a mile southward of the entrance and a cable westward of the alignment of the leading lights.

These lights consist of a low light on the Duty Officer's cabin on the Middle pier extremity and a high light at rear from a grey circular tower. The structures are conspicuous leading marks by day and the lights at night have a good range of visibility. Approach to the harbour is best made on their transit at 355°, but the Shoreham breakwater lights are not always easy to pick up against the background of bright lights. There is a red light (160 ft. elevation) on the third programme radio mast, situated about $1\frac{1}{4}$ cables NW of the high light. This is useful to steer for on a northerly bearing until the West breakwater light is identified.

The entrance lies between the two concrete breakwaters and within are east and west piers. Within these is a third pier (the Middle pier) on the fork of the Western and Eastern arms.

Off the entrance the west going stream starts about 2 hrs. before high water and the east going 6 hrs. later. During the west going stream there is a SW set across the entrance from the East breakwater towards the West breakwater, where part of it is deflected into the entrance and then NE towards the end of the East pier. The eddy is strongest 1 hr. before high water to ebb 1 hr. after high water. The maximum rate of the main stream at the harbour entrance is about 3 knots, but the flood sets into the Western arm where it can attain

---

4 knots, and the ebb 5 knots in some parts at springs. In the Eastern arm there is practically no stream, but a yacht should be piloted with caution in the vicinity of the division off the Middle pier.

The channel in the Eastern arm is dredged and leads to the locks into the Southwick canal. The Western arm is only suitable for visiting yachts, if able to take the ground. For dredged depths in both Arms see Plan No. 8. Vessels must keep well clear of dredgers. Traffic signals, given below, must be observed.

Traffic Signals Signals controlling the Eastern arm are exhibited from a mast 20 ft. east of the Middle pier lighthouse, and repeated at a mast on the northern side of the Prince George Lock.

A blue flag by day or a blue light at night signifies that no vessel shall proceed along Eastern arm for the purpose of leaving the harbour, moving to another berth in Eastern arm or passing into Western arm.

A red diamond by day, or, at night, a red Qk. Fl. light signifies that no vessel shall enter the harbour for the purpose of proceeding to Eastern arm, and no vessel outside the harbour shall be navigated in such a way as to hinder the passage of vessels leaving the harbour.

Two blue flags by day or two blue lights at night, all disposed vertically signify that no vessel shall navigate within the Eastern arm nor shall enter the harbour for the purpose of proceeding to Eastern arm.

Similar signals displayed from a mast 40 ft. west of the Middle pier lighthouse and at the mast to the northward have the same meanings but apply to the Western arm.

The above signals are purely negative, so yachts can enter or leave except when the prohibitory signals are exhibited. The Channel Pilot states in effect that while it may at times be necessary for the Harbour Master to regulate times of entry or departure a vessel once under way is under control of her master. However, the local Byelaws must be observed.

Signals at Locks No vessel may approach to enter the canal until a green pennant by day or a green light by night is exhibited at the outer end of the lock. Similarly no vessel may approach to leave until a yellow pennant by day or an amber light by night is exhibited near the inner end of the lock. If a black ball by day or a red light at night is exhibited no vessel may approach for the purpose of entering the lock or mooring at the lead-in. During non-tidal periods instructions must be taken from the duty officer on the Middle pier who will give permission for yachts to anchor close to the eastward side of the Middle pier.

Tidal Signals One ball at upper yard-arm indicates a depth of not less than 6 ft. above chart datum. Two balls at upper yard-arm 8–10 ft.; three balls at upper yard-arm 10–12 ft.; one ball at each yard-arm more than 12 ft. above chart datum. Low light (Middle pier) shows red when the tide level does not exceed 6 ft.

above chart datum; green when 6–10 ft. of water above chart datum; white when level is more than 10 ft. above chart datum.

Lights East breakwater light Fl. G. ev. 5 sec. 9 M. West breakwater light Fl. R. ev. 5 sec. 9 M. Leading lights (in line 355° true) high light (rear) Fl. W. ev. 10 sec. 12 M. Low light (front) Fixed W.R. or G. 10, 9, 9, M. (See tidal signals for change of colour.)

Fog Signals East breakwater siren ev. 2 min. Middle pier—Nauto ev. 20 sec. The latter is sounded when ships are approaching.

Anchorages etc. (1) Outside with offshore winds and settled weather in suitable depth of water, bottom mostly sand over clay or chalk. Note that the depths between the breakwaters vary from time to time. (2) Anchoring is not permitted in any part of the harbour without the permission of the Harbour Master except in emergency or for swinging. (3) As is usual in all British ports berthing arrangements are the responsibility of the Harbour Master, and instructions may be obtained from the Duty Officer at the Middle pier at all times. Before mooring at any wharf it is necessary to obtain the permission of the wharf owner concerned. The Harbour Authority is virtually without facilities of its own for the berthing of yachts. Whenever possible prior enquiry should be made to the local yards or clubs for berthing.

Western arm: James Taylor, Watercraft, Sussex Yacht, Lighthouse Club.

Eastern arm: Truslers, *Southwick canal:* Riverside Yard, Lady Bee, Sussex Yacht.

Facilities Water at yards or Sussex Yacht Club. Petrol and oil. All stores and chandlery adjacent to Southwick canal moorings. Yacht yards, gridiron, and scrubbing. Launching sites from beach, adjacent to high lighthouse and Middle pier, car park adjacent and muddy public hards throughout the harbour. Yacht Clubs: The Sussex Yacht Club. Sussex Motor Yacht Club has a club house on the south shore of the Western arm, approximately south-west of the Middle pier. Lighthouse Club. Trains and frequent buses to Brighton and elsewhere.

LITTLEHAMPTON

Plan No. 7

High Water (*Entrance*) +o h. o4 m. *Dover*.
Rise 16.6 *ft. springs;* 12.9 *ft. neaps*.
Depths *About* 1 *ft. at M.L.W.S. on bar, deepening between the piers to about* 5 *to* 8 *ft., which depths are maintained almost as far as the swing bridge*.

LITTLEHAMPTON is a convenient harbour for yachts except for the bar, which can only be crossed with sufficient rise of tide. Allowance has to be made for the strong streams in the entrance, and it is dangerous to approach in strong onshore winds. There is commercial shipping in the harbour and good facilities for yachts, with the town close by. Above the bridge the Arun River is navigable as far as Arundel, with a least depth of 5 ft. M.L.W.S. the whole way. The fixed railway bridge at Ford has 11 ft. clearance at H.W.

Approach and Entrance The harbour is situated 10 miles east of Selsey Bill. The entrance lies between two piers easily recognizable from seaward (see photograph) and 3 miles south-west is the Winter Knoll red can buoy. The western pier is the longer, and at its seaward end is a red barrel beacon. The eastern pier stops short at the esplanade, but there is a low dicker-work continuation built in the sands for about $\frac{1}{4}$ mile seawards. This is submerged from half tide to H.W., but is marked by perches with small top crosses and at its extremity by a beacon surmounted by a black diamond. The leading marks for the entrance are the lighthouse at the inshore end of the east breakwater and the outer light on a black steel column at the end of the short east breakwater in transit at 345°. The iron column may be only visible when in line and against the white background of the lighthouse. Keep nearer the eastern side when entering, if the tide is setting on to the western pier. The tide is very fierce up to narrow harbour entrance. It turns to west along the shore nearly 2 hrs. before H.W. Approach should not be attempted in strong onshore winds and on the ebb tide the entrance is rougher than at Shoreham as the streams are stronger. Newhaven is a better port of refuge.

Signals A pilot flag at the masthead means entrance prohibited, but vessels may leave during the signal.

Lights *East pier* front F. red 7 M. Rear Occ. W. Or. $7\frac{1}{2}$ sec. 10 M. White 287° to 000°; orange then to 042°. Lights in line 345°. *West pier* unwatched fixed white 6 M.

Anchorage (1) Outside, south of entrance at distance according to vessel's draft. This is slightly sheltered from the west by Selsey Bill and the Owers but is completely open from S.W., through S. to E.N.E. (2) Harbour Master allots moorings at berths on either side of the harbour. Yachts must be prepared to

30. *Littlehampton. River Arun at Arundel—bridge in background limits navigation although small motor cruisers proceed beyond it.*

take the mud (soft) at low water, except berths near the yacht-yards. Incoming yachts may anchor temporarily in the middle of the channel opposite Harbour Master's office (on starboard side of river opposite Arun Y.C.) and await berthing instructions. Dues to be paid at office.

Facilities Water at Harbour Master's, or from yards. Petrol and oil. All stores. Early closing day, Wednesday. Several yacht yards. Launching sites: light boats from hard sand foreshore on west side down river of the Arun Y.C. Yacht clubs: Arun Y.C., Littlehampton S. & M.B. Station. Good service of buses.

31. *Littlehampton approaching from west.*

32. *Littlehampton looking into entrance from south on leading line.*

33. *Littlehampton entrance showing starboard hand beacon and starboard hand posts marking underwater dickerwork. Main break-water on left of photo.*

34.   *Littlehampton harbour.*

35.   *Littlehampton. River Arun—the low railway bridge.*

36.   *Littlehampton entrance showing lighthouse and funfair (conspicuous).*

37.   *Littlehampton harbour. Harbour office to left of large crane. Visiting yachts anchor opposite office and await berthing instructions.*

43

CHICHESTER HARBOUR

Plan No. 9a and 9b

High Water Entrance +0 h. 12 m. Dover.
Rise 14.2 ft. springs; 11 ft. neaps.
Depths *There is a wide bar off the entrance with the shallowest part about ½ or ¾ mile offshore with patchdries about 1 ft. M.L.W.S. but depths in the vicinity of the bar may vary year by year. Within the harbour there is another bar with 7 ft. M.L.W.S. situated south-east of the Gardner buoy. Otherwise there is ample water in the main channels and 1½ fathoms in the channel below Bosham, and from 2 to 2½ fathoms off Itchenor.*

CHICHESTER HARBOUR is an ideal small boat centre. There is racing for all small classes and there are more sailing clubs than in any equal area of water on the south coast with the exception of Plymouth. The harbour is an interesting one with many channels to explore, and variety from the mud-banked creeks to the clean, sandy shores at the entrance. Bosham and Itchenor are both attractive villages, and altogether the harbour, though crowded, is well worth visiting. There is a speed limit of 6 knots within the harbour, and water skiing is prohibited.

Approach and Entrance The entrance to Chichester harbour lies some 8 miles west of Selsey Bill. There are extensive sands extending seawards on both sides of the entrance, named the West Pole and the East Pole. The approach leads across the bar, about ½ or ¾ mile offshore, which dries about 1 ft. M.L.W.S., or 3 ft. lowest water, but is being dredged. With strong onshore winds there is a very ugly sea on the bar, especially on the ebb when the approach can be dangerous.

When approaching from east or west keep well off shore until the Nab Tower bears 184° (S. 14° S. mag.). Then alter course to 001° (say N. by E. mag.) to the approach across the bar when the following marks will be identified.

Chichester buoy (black conical with triangle top mark) which is maintained during summer months from April until October in position 1.8 miles seaward of Treloar's hospital which bears 001° 30′. On approaching the buoy the leading marks on Eastoke Point will be seen and the vessel should be steered on their transit which leads close to the buoy. They consist of a tripod beacon, with black and white topmark, on the beach as a front mark which is brought into line with the black and white mark on the gable of Treloar's hospital, a prominent bungalow building on the west side of the entrance.

Once across the bar the water deepens. When Treloar's lies about ¼ mile ahead bear a little to the

38. *Chichester entrance—beacon in foreground lines up with white chimney in background for leading line. Breakwater and beacon at its end are recent.*

eastward to skirt the West Pole sands, just far enough to open up the line of sand running northwards along the west side of the entrance, and no more. In the actual entrance the deep water lies on the west side, the channel is narrow, and the tides run fiercely, with the dangerous Winner sand (covered at high water) blocking three-quarters of the apparent entrance on the eastward side. This is marked by two small black conical buoys, one on its south-west and the other on the north-west. The west shore is very steep-to when Treloar's comes abeam. Keep close to it.

Within the entrance the channel divides into two arms. One leads up slightly west of north to Emsworth, and is over 2 fathoms deep so far as a mile below Emsworth. The other arm bears round the north side of the Winner to the eastward and leads to Itchenor, the Bosham channel and to Dell Quay. This may be termed the main channel, but there is a shallow bar which has to be crossed with only 7 ft. at M.L.W.S., or 5 ft. lowest water.

To enter the main channel (after passing Hayling Island Sailing Club and Black Point on the west side) bear to starboard to leave the black north-west Winner buoy to starboard and the red Gardner buoy to port.

The course is then approximately east mag., leaving to port the red Stocker and Copyhold buoys and to starboard the black mid-Winner and north-east Winner, the latter situated off the sandy East Head. The inner bar or shoal with only 7 ft. M.L.W.S. or 5 ft. L.A.T., lies east of the narrows between the Gardner and north-west Winner buoys, and once it has been crossed the channel deepens again.

Just short of the Sand Head buoy the channel begins to alter from an easterly to a north-easterly direction. A white beacon on the wooded shore $1\frac{1}{2}$ miles distant may be brought in line with Stoke Clump, a conspicuous clump of trees on the distant downs, visible except on misty days. On this course a vessel will leave to port the Camber buoy (spherical R.W.H.S.) on the east side of the entrance to the Thorney channel, which should be given a wide berth when proceeding up the main channel. The channel is marked by perches, but these are mostly on the banks and should be given a wide berth. Most of the other buoys within the harbour are racing buoys.

When the white beacon and wooded shore are about $\frac{1}{2}$ mile distant the black conical Wear buoy will lie on the starboard bow. Alter course approximately to east mag. to leave this buoy fairly close to starboard and proceed up the next reach to the junction of the Bosham and Chichester channels. A red and white spherical buoy is moored at the entrance to Bosham

Lake, which is left well to port continuing up the main (Chichester) channel to Itchenor. This channel is deep almost as far as Longmore Pt. about a mile east of Itchenor. It then shallows but is marked by buoys.

The Bosham channel carries 9 ft. to within a cable or two of the village and is marked by perches and a R.W. buoy at the principal bend in the channel. The Emsworth channel is marked by perches, is wide and presents no difficulty.

The Thorney channel is straightforward. It is entered by leaving the Camber buoy to starboard, and then leaving Pilsey Island and beacon to port and a perch to starboard. Give both a wide berth.

Lights Leading lights at entrance. Low light (Qk. Fl. red) on breakwater end at Eastoke Point; rear light (Gp. Fl. 5, 30 sec.) has been established on the gable of Treloar's hospital. It has 3 sectors: white over approach transit, red to west, green to east. These lights lead to the entrance only. As the buoys within the harbour are unlit (but fitted with Scotchlite reflectors) strangers are advised not to attempt entrance at night.

Anchorages and Berthing (1) In westerly winds, just within the entrance, north of Black Point, on edge of mud flats off the entrance to Mengham Rythe. (2) Off East Head on the east side of harbour entrance. Pleasant anchorage in settled weather, but rather exposed except from south and east. (3) About a mile up the Emsworth channel off Mill Rythe, on which there is a yacht yard,

39. *Itchenor Hard. The Harbour Master's office is the low square building and the visitor's buoy is on left, to be used while waiting instructions from the Harbour Master.*

or $\frac{1}{2}$ to $\frac{3}{4}$ mile below Emsworth. Berths on pontoons Emsworth Yacht Harbour 5 ft., access 5 ft. M.H.W. neaps, 9 ft. M.H.W. springs. (4) In the Thorney channel off hard, protected from westerly winds. (5) At the entrance of Bosham Creek there is a visitors' mooring for large yachts, to the west of Deep End buoy. (6) At Itchenor visiting yachts up to 10 tons should moor temporarily at the visitors' buoy (white barrel with red band) off the Harbour Master's office. The Harbour Master will then allocate a vacant mooring which is usually available. (7) In the basin at Birdham Pool after passing through the locks. Near the canal entrance is a yacht club and a restaurant. To reach basin leave R.W.

buoy to port and B.W. perches to starboard. (8) In the Chichester Yacht Basin. Eastward of R.W. buoy through dredged channel marked on starboard hand by B.W. beacons with triangular topmarks.

Port Operation Port Operation and Information Service V.H.F. (F.M.) Radio Telephony. Details of these services are available from the Harbour Master's office, Itchenor. Tel: Birdham 301.

Facilities Several of the anchorages mentioned above are far away from facilities. At Emsworth, Bosham and Itchenor, water, petrol and provisions can be obtained. Early closing day, Itchenor and Emsworth, Wednesday; Bosham, Thursday. There are yacht yards at all three villages and at Sandy Point, Mengham Rythe, Mill Rythe and Dell Quay.

Launching sites from public hards at end of roads at Itchenor, Bosham and Emsworth, with car parks near by. Near H.W. at the north-east side of Hayling Bridge at the slipway administered by the Langston Sailing Club and also at Dell Quay. At Black Point *by permission* from the Hayling Island S.C. Yacht clubs: Birdham Y.C., Bosham S.C., Chichester Cruising Club (Itchenor), Chichester Y.C. (Birdham), Dell Quay S.C., Emsworth S.C., Hayling Island S.C., Itchenor S.C., Langston S.C., Mengham Rythe S.C., West Wittering S.C.

40. *Mengham Rythe showing the quay at high water.*

LANGSTON HARBOUR

High Water +0 h. 14 m. Dover.
Rise 13.4 ft. springs; 10.5 ft. neaps.
Depths *Water at entrance varies year by year but there is not less than 6 ft., except outside over the hook-shaped bar extending from the East Winner Sand. Within the harbour 1 to 2 fathoms in main channels.*

LANGSTON HARBOUR offers a fine area of water for dinghies and centreboard boats. There is also plenty of water for cruising yachts in the main channels, though there are no deep anchorages immediately off villages with facilities as in Chichester harbour, nor is it so well buoyed.

Approach and Entrance The entrance is just under 2 miles east of the Dolphin marking the gap in the submerged barrier off Southsea. The East Winner and the West Winner sands lie one on each side of the entrance and dry out over a mile seaward. The entrance may be located by a tall chimney standing on the west side of the channel.

The Fairway buoy lies about a mile offshore, roughly in line with the Horse Sand Fort at the end of Southsea

41. *Langston harbour and entrance. Picture taken from within harbour facing south. Sinah Lake to left.* [*Photo: Aero Films*]

Barrier and No Man's Fort off Seaview. It is a red can port hand buoy on the west side of the fairway. However, the danger in the approach lies ½ mile south and over a mile SE of this buoy, where there is a bar in the

49

shape of a hook extending from the East Winner sand. This is shown on the Admiralty charts and has depths as low as 5 ft. M.L.W.S., reported to be still shoaling. Once over this and between the Fairway buoy and the small black conical buoy close south of the drying part of the East Winner the depth in recent years is not less than 6 ft. The outer bar and the approaches to Langston Harbour are dangerous in strong onshore winds, especially near low water on the ebb, when they should be avoided.

From the Fairway buoy two dolphins will be seen on the west side of the harbour entrance. A course should be steered for a position midway between the dolphins and the Hayling Island shore. The edge of the channel on the east side is steep-to in places and thus constitutes a danger when the sands are covered at high water. When in the entrance with land on either side there is plenty of deep water, but the tides run very hard in this bottleneck. Once within the harbour alter course to the desired anchorage. Small yachts without masts can pass under Hayling road bridge (7 ft. clearance M.H.W.S.) to Chichester Harbour.

Lights Fairway buoy Gp. Fl. (2) ev. 10 sec. Outer beacon Qk. Fl.

Anchorage and Facilities The usual anchorage is Sinah Lake, which is just within the entrance on the east side. To enter Sinah Lake bear eastwards to the ferry pontoon which is left close to starboard. On the port hand will be left a section of Mulberry harbour stranded on the south-west of a large sandbank. At the entrance of Sinah Lake there is a bar with only a $\frac{1}{2}$ fathom at L.W., but beyond this there are depths from 1 to $1\frac{1}{2}$ fathoms, although the best positions are occupied by moorings. Apply at yacht yard to ascertain whether one is vacant and may be hired. At Sinah there is a small shop and inn. Ferries cross the harbour mouth, and there is an hourly bus service to Hayling village, where there is a post office, an hotel and several shops. Early closing Wednesday.

Large yachts can anchor in the main channel, and other anchorages may be found in the various channels. Launching sites from the foreshore at the end of the roads leading to the ferry on either side of the entrance, preferably at slack water as the tides run very hard. Car parks adjacent. Yacht clubs: Eastney C. Association on W side of entrance, Locks S.C. on creek just inside W side of entrance with a concrete slip to L.W. Eastney Lake to the SE of the club will become a locked marina for 1,000 boats. Tudor S.C. on W of Broom channel, Langston S.C.

PORTSMOUTH HARBOUR

High Water +o *h.* 14 *m. Dover.*
Rise 13.4 *ft. springs;* 10.5 *ft. neaps.*
Depths *The entrance and main harbour is a deep ship channel. The Fareham channel has 4 to 5 fathoms at the entrance, gradually shallows, and there is little water off Fareham; Portchester channel is also deep at the entrance, and there is a fathom as far up as Portchester Castle.*

PRIMARILY a naval port, Portsmouth is not without interest from a yachting point of view. No city is better equipped to build or repair yachts, whether large or small, sail or power. It is a safe and convenient port, and the upper reaches and channels provide good small boat sailing and racing.

Approach and Entrance From the eastward the approach is simple, being buoyed for big ships and is shown on the chart. From the westward Gilkicker Point should be given a good berth. To keep in deep water, the Spit Sand Fort should be left ¼ mile to port, when course may be altered to the Spit Refuge buoy, whence leaving this to port the deep channel will be followed. A short cut across the Spit Sand, giving 8 ft. at low water, can be found ½ mile west of Spit Sand Fort, by keeping the high monument on the Southsea shore in line with St. Jude's Church at 49° (N.E. by E.¼E. mag.). Another swashway, available at high water but giving less than ½ fathom at

42. *Portsmouth entrance.*

low water, exists across the Hamilton bank by keeping the eastern side of the round tower on east of harbour entrance in line with the western side of a conspicuous tank at 26° (N.E.¾N. mag.).

In the entrance itself the tides are very strong, and sailing yachts will find it difficult under contrary conditions. The flood runs easy for 3 hrs., strong for 4 hrs.; the ebb easy 1 hr., strong for from 2 to 3 hrs., and then easy.

Vessels approaching inshore from the eastward may still pass through the gap in the submerged barrier. The gap is about a mile south of Lumps Fort and is marked by a pile on the north side and a dolphin (Qk. Fl.R) on the south. Many of the piles on the barrier have been removed, but the remains still constitute a danger.

Fareham Lake About 1½ miles from the entrance, Portsmouth harbour divides into two channels. The westward of the two is Fareham lake. On the eastern side of the entrance to this creek there are large stagings known as the Reserve Flagship Dolphins. A number of mooring buoys are placed on the starboard side in the first reach, and above this the channel is marked by posts on the mud on either bank; red posts to port, black to starboard. Where the Portchester channel joins the Fareham channel, do not mistake the first porthand (red) in the Portchester creek for a Fareham mark. At the end of the channel—over 3

miles up—is the town of Fareham, but for a mile below this there is little depth at low tide. This part of the channel is not shown on Plan No. 11 beyond the prohibited anchorage, where Heavy Reach turns westward for over ½ mile before turning northward towards Fareham. The channel continues to be marked by piles.

Portchester Lake This is the eastern arm referred to above. It is a wide channel, running near the entrance in a north-easterly direction, but there are several bends to be negotiated before it leads to the village of Portchester and the ruins of the castle of the same name. The navigation marks are the same as in Fareham creek, by posts; red posts port, black starboard.

Lights The approach and entrance to Portsmouth harbour are, of course, clearly marked by lights, which are shown on the chart. There are also lights within the harbour as far as the mouth of Fareham Lake.

Signals Signals are displayed at Central Signal Station, Fort Blockhouse, or Gilkicker Signal Station or in H.M. ships as appropriate.

1. *Day*. Red flag with white diagonal bar. *Night*. Red light over two white lights vertical. No vessel is to leave or enter the harbour channel, or approach N of Outer Spit buoy.

2. *Day*. Red flag with white diagonal bar over one black ball. No vessel is to enter Portsmouth

43.   *Portsmouth entrance and conspicuous power station as seen approaching from south-west over Spit Sand.*

44.   *Portsmouth from Gosport showing conspicuous new block of flats, the power station and entrance of Camber.*

harbour channel from seaward. Outgoing traffic from Portsmouth may proceed.

3. *Day*. Red flag with white diagonal bar over two black balls. No outgoing vessel is to leave Portsmouth harbour. Ingoing traffic may use Portsmouth harbour channel and enter Portsmouth harbour.

4. *Day*. Large black pendant. *Night*. White light over two red lights vertical. No vessel to anchor in the Man-of-War anchorage at Spithead.

5. *Day*. International Code Pendant superior to ZV. *Night*. Red light foremast. H.M. ship entering, leaving or shifting berth. Keep clear.

6. *Day*. International Code Pendant superior to ZU. Warning Major War Vessel under way.

7. *Day*. Flags TF. *Night*. Green over red light. You should proceed with great caution at easy speed. (Signal from Blockhouse Signal Station, when ships leave the Camber.)

8. Spit drum. Precautionary signal when weather is bad at Spithead and it may be dangerous for boats to leave the harbour.

9. *Day*. Flag E. *Night*. Red light submarine, entering or leaving Haslar lake.

10. *Day*. Red flag with white St. Andrew's cross. *Night*. Two red lights horizontal. Have divers down.

Anchorage, etc. (1) Camber on eastern side of entrance. It is sometimes possible to lie beside the dock wall afloat for short periods, but only with permission. The Camber is now a very busy commercial dock for coaster traffic and in addition the new I.W. car ferry terminus is built over the old 'Dirty Corner' fishing harbour. Unless there is some particular reason for entering it the Camber is no longer a practical yacht berth. (2) Off Gosport at the Marina on application to the Marina office (blue and yellow hut) on the quay. There is also Camper & Nicholson's new marina, and moorings for large yachts off their yards, for which application should be made at the yard or to the launchman. Caution: between Camper & Nicholson's and the Marina there is a spit of gravel extending from the shore. (3) Haslar lake, the creek on west side of entrance. Permission to enter this must be obtained from Queen's Harbour Master. Lie on moorings. Depths $1\frac{1}{2}$ to $3\frac{1}{2}$ fathoms in entrance. Small power boats pass under bridge, where there is more room. (4) Off the Hardway, which is situated on port hand near the entrance to Fareham lake. Note the concrete hard and pontoon landing stage are the only public landings in the vicinity. The piers are either Admiralty or Vosper's property. (5) In Bombketch and Spider lakes. (6) In Fareham lake above Bedenham pier in $1\frac{1}{2}$ fathoms, or on moorings in the bend, about $\frac{1}{2}$ mile below Fareham in about 1 fathom. (7) In Portchester lake in about 1 fathom near the castle, if a mooring is available. If no mooring is free, anchor as near to the castle as possible clear of moorings.

Facilities At Gosport and Portsmouth every facility for yachts is available. Fuels, chandlery and water *on tap*, at Camber, Gosport Marina and Hardway. Yachts to 8 ft. draught may be scrubbed on the concrete hard at Hardway. There are several yacht yards and two leading sailmakers. Early closing day, Wednesday; Southsea, Saturday. Fareham also can provide yachts with most necessaries, and there are boat builders. Early closing is also on Wednesday. There is only a village at Portchester, but petrol and provisions are obtainable (early closing, Wednesday), and there is a small boat-yard where rope and small necessaries can be supplied. Frequent buses to Portsmouth from Fareham and Portchester. Stations at Fareham and Portchester. Express service from Portsmouth harbour or town station. Launching sites: (1) Portsmouth from car ferry slipway providing ferry is not obstructed. (2) Gosport from hard adjacent to Marina office, with car parking room near. (3) Portchester from hard at end of road near castle with parking limited. (4) Fareham at public slipway next to Chippendale Boats Ltd., 3 hrs. each side H.W. (5) Hardway at hard adjacent to sailing club. (6) At hard at Gosport Cruising Club 3 hrs. each side H.W. Yacht clubs: R. Albert Y.C., R.N.S.A., Portsmouth S.C., Hardway S.C., Portsbridge C.C., Portchester S.C., Fareham S. & M.B.C., Gosport C.C.

45.   *Gosport yacht marina and Camper & Nicholson's yard on left. The picture faces north-west.*

BEMBRIDGE HARBOUR

Plan No. 12

High Water +0 h. 14 m. Dover.
Rise 13.4 ft. springs; 10.5 ft. neaps.
Depths *There is a bar at the entrance with zero soundings. Within the harbour there are depths up to 5 ft., but the water is impounded from 1 hr. before to 2 hrs. after L.W. giving about an extra 2 ft. above datum.*

BEMBRIDGE is a charming harbour and conveniently situated for the east end of the island. The marked channel is approached from the eastward and lies to the south of St. Helen's Fort. The entrance is protected from westerly and southerly winds. A great handicap is the lack of room for visiting yachts and the shallowness of the harbour. The buoyage and lights have been maintained principally for the pilots, who are now based at Ryde. It is now best to enter only during daylight on a flood tide and to exercise caution, until improvements are made. Bembridge could be converted into a first rate yacht harbour.

Approach and Entrance The approach to Bembridge harbour may be identified by St. Helen's Fort which lies about 5 cables offshore, east of Nodes Point.

The fort is surrounded by breakwater rocks and ½ cable distance off the east side should be the limit of approach. When approaching from the north do not attempt to pass inside (west of) the fort.

The approach is south of St. Helen's Fort towards St. Helen's seamark (tower on shore). The entrance is well buoyed, No. 1 buoy, black with light (starboard hand) lies about 1 cable W.S.W. of the fort. The course then leads past buoys 2, 4, 6 to port and 3, 5, 7 to starboard and turning to port at No. 6 (red fixed light), carefully following small port hand buoys (red/white bands), continue and pass No. 8 port hand buoy giving about 40 yds. clearance as there is a steep sandy spit here on which the buoy dries at half tide.

Lights St. Helen's Fort Gp. Fl. (3) 10 sec., 7 M. 53 ft. elevation. No. 1 buoy flash ev. sec., No. 6 buoy flashing red. Light beacon situated on St. Helen's shore south of sea mark is a red, white, green sector light, the white sector giving the line of approach as far as No. 6 buoy only. In 1967 the lights on the buoys were only occasionally shown and the leading lights up the channel were discontinued.

Moorings and Anchorage Boats should not obstruct the buoyed fairway which leads to St. Helen's quay. Should any craft anchor near fairway an anchor light is required. The area south of St. Helen's Fort is officially a prohibited anchorage owing to the presence of cables. If compelled to anchor for any reason while waiting for the tide off No. 1 buoy it is essential that the anchor should be buoyed to avoid fouling. Clear ground may be found 1½ cables north-east of the fort outside the prohibited anchorage area, and there is a good outside anchorage farther eastward ½ mile north-west of the lifeboat station, protected from south-west. There is a stone hard and a number of moorings are laid for local yachts. Anchor clear of these, and here also it is a wise precaution to buoy the anchor.

When inside the harbour apply for a mooring temporarily and report to the Harbour Master, Mr. Attrill (Bembridge 2319). Large craft should proceed direct to St. Helen's quay where the bottom is soft mud. Landings may be made on the beach near the Spithead Hotel or the beach at St. Helen's Duver or at marine works (by leading lights).

Facilities Fuel, chandlery, etc. from Mr. Wade, marine works, near leading lights. There are several good yacht yards. Buses to all parts of the Island. Hotels, small shops. Early closing day, Thursday. Yacht clubs: Bembridge S.C., Brading Haven Y.C. Launching site: from yacht yards by arrangement.

46. *Bembridge No. 1 Buoy.*

Plan No. 13

High Water (*Cowes*) + 0 h. 12 m. *Dover*.
Rise 11.8 *ft. springs;* 9.3 *ft. neaps*.
Depths *The channel is dredged to 8 ft. up to the ferry slipway. In the river there is only from a ¼ to ½ fathom.*

WOOTTON CREEK is pretty and for small craft the entrance is normally easy to identify and navigate. Like other sailing ports it suffers from over-popularity, resulting in difficulty in finding room to bring up, though facilities have recently been improved.

Approach and Entrance The entrance to the creek, the channel of which is clearly marked by four beacons, lies south of south-east Ryde Middle buoy (red and white chequered). Strangers should steer from the northward for the outside beacon, leaving this and the others to starboard. The dredged channel is very narrow, and when the yacht comes between Fishbourne and the fourth beacon she must alter course towards the westward shore, and if proceeding up river pick up the leading marks in line which consist of two white triangles on the foreshore near a boathouse. The channel above the leading marks is marked by perches and yachts at moorings give an additional indication of its trend.

If proceeding to the bight off the ferry hard, which is usual for visitors, continue up the 8 ft. dredged channel from No. 4 beacon to just off the end of the staging at the ferry hard, before turning into the anchorage.

Lights No. 1 and 3 beacons Fl. ev. 6 sec. No. 2 and 4 beacons Fl. G. ev. 6 sec.

Anchorage The creek is usually rather crowded in the summer months. The usual anchorage is in the bight beyond the ferry pier. Here there has been considerable silting and the depth is little over 2 ft. M.L.W.S., but yachts sit upright in very soft mud. Anchors should be buoyed and it is essential to anchor clear of the ferry fairway. Ferries now run all night Fridays and Saturdays. There are also moorings but it is best to obtain advice from Mr. Young, the berthing master, who usually meets incoming yachts and directs them to a berth.

To the west and north is a dangerous finger of mud which separates the dredged bight from the main channel.

Shallow draft vessels will find room to anchor up river in $\frac{1}{4}$ fathom L.W., but there are many moorings in the best parts. Advice can be obtained from the berthing master.

Facilities At Fishbourne there is an inn and garage, and the R. Victoria Y.C. club house. This combines the former three separate clubs in one practical new building, with hard, car park, changing rooms, bar and club boatman—an example which could usefully be followed in other harbours. Visiting yachts welcome and temporary membership available to members of recognized yacht clubs. At Wootton, $\frac{3}{4}$ mile up the river or a mile's walk from Fishbourne, there is Please's yacht yard and garage (water and petrol), P.O., shops, inn. Early closing Thursday. Launching sites: from ferry hard or yacht club by arrangement. Frequent buses from Wootton bridge to Ryde and Newport.

47. *The course from the fourth beacon is direct to the end of the ferry pier and then to starboard into the anchorage in the bight. The shallow spit to be avoided lies to the right of the yacht on extreme right of picture extending northwards, then eastwards between the river itself and the fairway to ferry hard.*

48. *Wootton Creek from the anchorage in the bight at Fishbourne facing north-east towards the car ferry terminal.*

49. *Wootton Creek from Fishbourne looking at west shore across yacht anchorage.*

COWES

Plan No. 14

High Water *Mean difference:* +0 h. 12 m. Dover.
Rise 11.8 ft. springs; 9.3 ft. neaps.
Depths *The channel is dredged 8½ ft., but there has been a tendency to silt. There is between 1 and 2 fathoms as far as 1½ miles beyond the floating bridge.*

COWES remains the principal yachting port of the British Isles, and is the headquarters of the Royal Yacht Squadron. It is a town of tradition and character that time has little changed. Situated in the centre of the Island coast opposite the entrance of Southampton Water, it is the most conveniently placed harbour in the Solent. There is always room to bring up, and the harbour is well protected except from the northward.

Approach and Entrance The entrance is a particularly simple one and well marked. The fairway lies on the west side of the entrance, and is marked by the port hand R.W. (No. 4) light buoy and the starboard hand black conical (No. 3) buoy; in the harbour there are two red port hand buoys.

Approaching from the east, keep outside a line from Old Castle buoy to the Royal Yacht Squadron castle,

50.   *West Cowes from East Cowes.*

Visitors Moorings

Private Moorings

Pontoon

51. *Facing south over Cowes Harbour. Fairway on right (west) side of river, moorings for local and racing yachts on left and trots of moorings for visiting yachts on starboard side of fairway beyond the pontoon with steamer alongside. [Photo: Aero Films]*

which stands out conspicuously on the north-west corner of the entrance. This is in order to avoid the Shrape Mud, a large shoal extending across the harbour mouth from the east side. A long breakwater extends across the Shrape bank, with the object of forcing the tide to scour the channel, thus preventing silting. There is little water to the north and east of this breakwater. A special Hovercraft fairway on the east side of the harbour and close round the end of the breakwater is marked by orange buoys. Yachts crossing this channel should exercise caution.

Approaching from the west, there is deep water a cable offshore but there are ledges of rock east of Egypt Point and off the shore along Cowes Green to the Royal Yacht Squadron. Leave No. 3 outer black buoy to starboard. Note that an early flood or ebb which runs contrary to the main tide will be found close to the esplanade by the Royal Yacht Squadron.

The Victoria pier has been demolished, but foul ground containing rocks is left in the vicinity.

There is a speed limit of 7 knots, but yachts must slow down below this in vicinity of other yachts on moorings or as seamanship requires.

Lights The Prince Consort buoy, north-east of the entrance, exhibits a flashing light, and there is a light (Fl. red ev. 5 sec.) on the outer (No. 4) port hand buoy. A red group flashing (2) light is placed on the end of the eastern breakwater. New leading lights at 164° have recently been established: Front Iso. 2 sec., Rear Iso. red 2 sec. The rear red light is visible 120° to 240° north to 060°.

Anchorage Large yachts anchor in the roads outside to the north of the Shrape bank, or occasionally off Cowes esplanade. Two or three visitor's moorings are laid off Cowes esplanade for short period use. The trots of harbour board moorings where visiting yachts berth alongside each other are placed on the west side of the harbour beyond the pontoon. A number of private moorings are placed in the 6 ft. of water southward of the end of the eastern breakwater and should not be used without permission of the Harbour Master. During Cowes Week additional moorings are laid for the various classes of competing yachts. There are a few visitor's pile moorings above White's yard in the Medina River and other moorings in the river, but not much room for anchoring without obstructing the fairway for commercial shipping. The river is perfectly sheltered, and there are 1¾ to 2 fathoms of water so far as the beacons on the east side marking the measured mile. Several new schemes for marina type berthing are under consideration and amenities are likely to be improved.

Facilities Every kind of yachting requirement is catered for. There are yacht yards, sailmakers, brokers, yacht chandlers, and many shops of all kinds. Early closing day is on Wednesday. Frequent motor buses. Ferry steamer and Hovercraft to Southampton. Yacht clubs: Royal Yacht Squadron, R. London Y.C., R. Corinthian Y.C., Island S.C., East Cowes S.C., Cowes Corinthian Y.C. Launching sites: (1) From the slipway off the esplanade near Island Sailing Club, with car park adjacent. (2) From the slipway on town quay adjacent to the ferry pontoon, but car parking restricted. (3) Heavy boats can be craned into the water from British Road Service jetty by arrangement.

HAMBLE RIVER

Plan No. 15

High Water (*Mean*) —0 h. 19 m. *Dover.*
Rise 12.3 ft. springs; 9.7 ft. neaps.
Depths 2¼ fathoms in entrance, and from 3 fathoms to 1½ fathoms in the channel as far as Port Hamble. Above this 1½ fathoms will be found to within a cable or so below Bursledon bridge, and in places this depth is exceeded.

THE HAMBLE RIVER owes its popularity as a yachting centre to its convenience. Situated at the entrance of Southampton Water, it is a good harbour from which cruises may be made to the various Solent and other ports, and provides a base for many offshore and racing yachts of all classes. The channel is available at all states of the tide, and the river's only disadvantage is that owing to popularity it has become overcrowded.

Approach and Entrance On coming abreast of Calshot castle alter course to 350° true (north mag.). The vessel will leave to starboard the Hook pillar bell buoy (which is situated in the centre of Southampton Water) and the course leads to Hamble Point buoy (spherical B.W.H.S.).

When approaching from the eastward keep well offshore, leaving the Coronation buoy close to starboard and not steering east of Hamble Point buoy until this is close at hand.

52.   *After sailing up the channel with mud flats on either hand, the entrance of the river proper is between the point with Fairey Marine sheds shown in the photograph and the pier which is out of the picture on the right. The fairway is on starboard side.*

Hamble Point buoy marks the southern extremity of a sand and mud spit on the west side of the Hamble River. The spit dries out for a considerable distance at L.W. and on the east side of the river there is an almost equally large expanse of mud.

Leave Hamble buoy to port, and a series of posts will be seen. Four to be left to port are red with can-shaped topmarks, and to starboard there are five black piles with triangle tops. The first reach leading up between the piles on either hand can be taken on a bearing of 345° true (N. ½ W.) with the gable of a conspicuous house just open of the second port-hand pile, where the channel takes a bend to the north-east towards the end of Warsash pier. However, the piles mark the channel very clearly, but near the entrance the best water lies to starboard. Do not pass too close to the piles.

In the river itself the channel is obvious, as there are always yachts and boats moored on each side.

It is the turn in the channel that misleads strangers, and makes navigation difficult at night. When approaching Hamble Point buoy the inner river entrance by Warsash can be seen, but it must not be steered for until the second red port-hand pile has been passed.

Lights Hamble Point buoy Gp. Fl. (3) ev. 15 sec. Second port-hand pile situated at bend in river Gp. occ. (2) ev. 12 sec. Two red lights at Warsash pier. One red light at R.T.Y.C. pier a farther ¼ mile up the river.

Anchorage Except in the entrance below No. 9 starboard-hand pile there is no room for anchoring.

53.   *Warsash as seen coming into Hamble River.*

Most of the river is occupied by pile moorings. The following berths may be used by visiting yachts, and are subject to the usual harbour board dues. *Warsash.* Piles or buoys on the port hand opposite Tormentor yard. *Hamble.* Abreast the 'Ditty Box' (see photograph) there are moorings for large yachts and on the starboard side certain of the pile moorings are allocated to visitors. In the absence of the owners berths are sometimes available at Hamble Marina, on the port hand above the yard, on application to the Marina Harbour Master. *Lower Swanwick.* Buoys on the port hand opposite Universal Shipyards Ltd. *Bursledon.* Piles on the port hand opposite the Jolly Sailor. Berths may be available at Swanwick Marina, on the starboard hand. The berths at mooring piles in the river are mostly private, being rented on an annual basis but berths may be available on application to the Harbour Master or at yacht yards.

Facilities There are small shops and post offices at Hamble, Warsash, Bursledon and Swanwick. Early closing day is Wednesday, except at Warsash where it is on Thursday. At Hamble there is a yacht yard, with yacht chandlery and sailmaker. At Warsash, Bursledon and Swanwick there are also good yards, engine repairers and yacht chandlers. Water and petrol may be obtained from the supply boats operating in the river and at the yacht yards. In addition yachts can go alongside the 'Ditty Box' at Hamble and at the pontoon at the Tormentor yard at Warsash for fuel and water. Launching sites: (1) Warsash public hard, car park adjacent. (2) Hamble public hard, car park adjacent. (3) Swanwick Shore public hard (next to Moody's yacht yard) with car park adjacent. (4) At Bursledon, Land's End public hard with car park at station ¼ mile distant. Buses from Warsash, Hamble, Swanwick and Bursledon. Station at Bursledon. Yacht clubs: R. Southern Y.C., R. Thames Y.C., Hamble River S.C., Warsash S.C.

54. *Port Hamble. The 'Ditty Box' (black hull, white upperworks) for petrol, water, etc. is moored at the end of the pier.*

SOUTHAMPTON

Plan No. 16 & 17

High Water (*Mean*) +0 h. 24 m. Dover.
Rise 13 *ft. springs;* 10.5 *ft. neaps.*
Depths *Deep harbour for ships of any size.*

SOUTHAMPTON WATER is a natural harbour which has been used by ships of all kinds from time immemorial. It is an almost straight stretch of water, measuring some 6 miles from Calshot castle to the Royal pier.

Navigation is easy in any weather bar fog, and there are anchorages available for yachts. So far as facilities are concerned the town provides everything that can possibly be required by yachtsmen. It is an easy journey from London.

Approach and Entrance When entering Southampton Water strangers will, of course, be navigating from a chart of the Solent. It will be seen that the main channel lies between Calshot Spit lightship (shortly to be replaced again by a buoy) and Calshot Pillar buoy, and runs north-west close to Calshot castle. Yachts approaching from the west may take a short cut over the end of Calshot Spit in 1¼ fathoms low water, by leaving Calshot Spit lightship ½ cable to starboard and

55.   *Fawley jetty as seen from deep channel when coming up Southampton Water.*

steering for Black Jack buoy (off Calshot castle) leaving this to port or very close to starboard.

Approaching from the eastward keep well offshore between Hill Head and Hamble, as the shoal water extends a surprisingly long way from the shore. Whether coming from east or west remember the Bramble Bank, situated in mid-Solent. In spite of being such a well-known danger, many yachts still go ashore on it.

Once within Southampton Water navigation is easy. Mud flats run off a long way on the western side, and on the eastern side at the southern end (Hamble Spit and Bald Head) and the northern end (East Mud). The deep ship channel is marked by red buoys on the west side, and by black conical buoys on the east side.

The docks will be seen from a considerable distance. Here there is a junction of two channels, the Test River leading approximately north-west, and the Itchen River joining from N.N.E. The Test is the main channel leading past the ocean docks, the Royal pier and the long line of the new docks. Note that parallel with the docks south of the Town quay is the 'Gymp' shoal. Keeping on the east side of the river, the Gymp buoys marking the shoal will be left to port. Above the Royal pier there is the deep-dredged channel along the new docks on the east side, but beyond the pier yachts keep to the south-west side, leaving Cracknore buoy to port, to proceed up the Marchwood channel of the River Test. There is a ½ fathom shoal between No. 6 red fairway buoy and the beacon north-east of Marchwood pier but the rest of the channel carries over 1 fathom as far as Leek Bed, above which it is navigable with sufficient rise of tide as far as Eling. The docks are being extended from King George V dock to the N.W., which will affect the area and buoyage west of Marchwood.

The Itchen is a deep channel to within ½ mile of Northam bridge. At the entrance liners of average size lie alongside the docks, and beyond these are various basins for smaller commercial vessels. The big ship-building yards of Thornycrofts and Camper & Nicholson's are situated on the banks of the Itchen channel.

Lights Calshot Spit lightship exhibits a light Fl. ev. 5 sec. (shortly to be replaced by a buoy), and the Calshot Pillar buoy, Fl. ev. 3 sec., bell ev. 30 sec. The entrance between the two is thus as easy by night as by day. Southampton Water is marked by buoys with R. occ. or flashing lights on the west and white flashing or occ. lights on the east. The lights are so numerous that reference to chart and light list should be made.

Anchorages *Hythe.* Large yachts lie north and south of Hythe pier. Smaller craft find moorings, or anchor south of the pier. Yacht yard, hotel, shops, petrol etc. Early closing, Wednesday. *Southampton.* There are harbour board moorings for large yachts off the Royal pier. *Marchwood.* There is anchorage above the pier in 1 to 2 fathoms with landing at the public magazine hard. *River Itchen*. This is not a very suitable place for bringing up, unless proceeding to one of the yacht yards. Moorings are available and there is room to anchor in some parts (buoy anchor to avoid fouling moorings and avoid prohibited areas).

Facilities Southampton, like Portsmouth, provides facilities of every kind for vessels large or small. There are shipbuilders, yacht builders, dinghy builders, engineers, sailmakers, ship chandlers and shops of all kinds. Early closing days are Mondays or Wednesdays. Hotels. Express trains from Southampton Central. Bus services to all parts. Coaches. Launching sites: (1) From the foreshore at Hythe. (2) Weston shore. (3) Eling Creek hard. (4) Netley public hard. Yacht clubs: R. Southampton Y.C., Southampton S.C., Eling S.C., Weston S.C., Hythe S.C., Marchwood Y.C.

56.   *Southampton Docks as seen approaching—River Itchen on right, River Test on left.*

BEAULIEU RIVER

High Water (*Mean*) +o h. 12 m. *Dover.*
Rise 10 *ft. springs; 8 ft. neaps.*
Depths *About ¾ fathom on the bar at L.W.; in the reaches up to the turn before Buckler's Hard there is 1 to 1½ fathoms though the bottom is uneven with deep pools and also a 5 ft. shoal in the first reach, a 3 ft. shoal about 2 cables south-east of Gin's Farm. A depth of ¾ fathom is maintained past Buckler's Hard and almost as far as the brick works.*

BEAULIEU RIVER provides one of the most beautiful anchorages within the Solent. A long, straight channel leads between the mud flats to the river proper, most of which lies between deep woods on either hand. The entrance is not difficult, and is available to most vessels except at exceptionally low spring tides.

Approach and Entrance From the west follow the line of the Hampshire coast, keeping well away from the mud flats, until the Lepe Coastguard Station and a

57. *Entrance of Beaulieu River.*

boat-house to the east of the entrance bear about north. The marks for the entrance will then be seen. There is a red dolphin with small reflective barrel-shaped (from seaward) topmark marking the eastern extremity of Beaulieu Spit, which is left about 15 yds. to port. The leading beacons which should be brought into line consist of white boards: the front (or lower) one on the first port hand boom (a red pile) and the rear (or high one) on shore backed by the dark green trees at 337°. As the shore is approached there is a sharp turn in the channel towards W.S.W. The entrance and lower channel are marked by 8 red piles with small red reflectors and can-

shaped topmarks on the port side, and by 7 black piles with white reflectors and cone topmarks on the starboard. Up river of the piles there are perches.

From the eastward make 2 cables west of the East Lepe buoy, and when the coastguard station and boat-house are recognized alter course towards them until the leading marks are identified, when proceed as before at 337°.

The entrance is clearly marked, but no short cuts must be taken as the outer beacon stands on the mud flats, and opposite it on the east side of the rather narrow entrance channel the water is very shallow.

58.   *Beaulieu River. Gilbury Hard and pier as seen coming up river. (Pier is private.)*

Whether coming from east or west keep well offshore, and approach the beacon and the leading marks on a course between N. and N.N.E.

Once beyond the first bend, the channel is marked on both sides by perches and it is fairly wide. There are two shoals in the first reach, a 3 ft. shoal two cables south-east of Gin's Farm and another on the west side of the channel off Gin's Farm.

Lights None.

Anchorage The area in which to anchor is restricted owing to the large number of moorings. Yachts may anchor only in the long reach between the entrance and Need's Oar Point. At Buckler's Hard there is a trot of pile moorings for visitors and other moorings can some-times be had on application to the Harbour Master.

Facilities Water and petrol are laid on at the pier at Buckler's Hard. Here there is an hotel. Provisions and deep freeze can be obtained from the small store which keeps open late except on Thursdays and there is also a taxi service. Yacht yard facilities at Marine Services yacht Yard. Launching site at Buckler's Hard or from beach at Lepe opposite the entrance to the river; both with convenient car parks. Yacht clubs: Beaulieu River S.C. and R. Southampton Y.C. at Ginn's Farm. Occasional bus service. Nearest station Beaulieu Road, 6 miles. At Exbury on the other side of the river there is a small grocers, a post office and a garage.

59.
Beaulieu River.
Buckler's Hard and
pier on right with
public landing,
petrol, etc.

NEWTOWN RIVER

Plan No. 19

High Water (*Mean*) — o h. 20 m. *Dover.*
Rise *Approximately:* 9 ft. springs; 6½ ft. neaps.
Depths *From* 3 *to* 4 *ft. on the bar; sometimes less; once across the bar the depths increase to* 1¾ *to* 2 *fathoms as far as the junction with Clamerkin Lake. Above this there is a fathom or over for* ¼ *mile, after which the depths decrease rapidly.*

THE VILLAGE of Newtown is one of the smallest in the Isle of Wight. Once it was the capital, and vessels of all sizes used the river as a harbour. Romans sacked the town, and then in 1377 it was burnt to the ground by the French. Today there is little except the old town hall (now National Trust property) and cuttings through the trees, where once ran roads, to hint of its former importance. But the river still remains, and where once lay fourteenth century sailing ships one now sees yachts and boats. It is still the least spoilt of the Solent harbours and, although the anchorage is often crowded during weekends, the river, the marshlands and woods retain much of their original character.

Approach and Entrance The entrance to New-town River is 3½ miles east of Yarmouth and lies eastward of Hamstead Point, which is the most pro-nounced headland between Yarmouth and Gurnard. It will be identified with certainty when the Hamstead Ledge black conical buoy is sighted. The bar lies ¾ mile E.S.E. of this buoy.

As the entrance is approached the leading marks will be seen, although they are not very conspi-cuous. They stand on the shore east of the entrance and consist of two posts, the outer one having a Y topmark and the inner one a white disc surrounded by a black ring. Alter course to stand in on these marks, and allow for strong athwart ship tide. Leave the bar buoy (red spherical) to port and the second (black spherical, marking a gravel spit projecting towards the channel) to starboard. When the Y post is close ahead alter course for the entrance between the shingle points. There are a few perches on each side of the channel, and here the tide conforms to the direction of the channel, running either in or out.

Soon the entrance will be at hand. To starboard there is a shingle spit which is fairly steep-to, but beyond it is mud, whilst on the port hand a little farther in is another fairly steep shingle point, known as Fishhouse Point. Beyond this the channel divides; the port-hand one is Clamerkin Lake, but the main chan-nel is straight ahead and runs in a southerly direction.

60. *Newtown looking across entrance from west side towards Clamerkim Lake—starboard hand perch on extreme left, main channel on right.*

73

There is a nasty reef of gravel to starboard opposite the junction of Clamerkin Lake and the main river, so keep to port after entering, before sweeping round into the centre of the river. In this reach there are usually yachts on moorings or at anchor which show the lie of the channel, and a few perches. Here the channel is very narrow at L.W.

Anchorage The anchorage is between the junction of the main channel with Clamerkin Lake (where there is 9 ft.) and the junction with Causeway Lake $\frac{1}{4}$ mile farther south, where there is about 5 ft. at low water. Several moorings occupy the best positions in about 8 ft. M.L.W.S., so that the visitor will have to anchor where best he can, nearer the entrance according to what space is available. The anchorage is rather exposed to north-east winds. Alternatively, there is nearly always room in Clamerkin Lake where there is always 6 ft. of water at low tide for a considerable distance. Moorings can often be hired on application to the Harbour Master. Small dues are charged to help with cost of upkeep of river and moorings; if not collected put a suitable coin in the box beside the boathouse. Smaller craft that do not mind taking the mud at low water will find room farther up the main channel. There are no lights on the river at night.

Facilities Farm produce can be obtained at the farms at Lower Hamstead, Shalfleet or Newtown, but there are no shops at Newtown.

Water can be obtained by courtesy at the farms or cottages. There is no station or bus service at Newtown. Row up to Shalfleet quay (boatyard and petrol) and it is a pleasant walk to Shalfleet where there is a bus service to Newport and Yarmouth. Shalfleet is 2 miles from the anchorage. Here there is a small shop and inn, and petrol may be obtained. If possible, row up on the flood and return on the ebb.

61.   *Yarmouth from the castle, showing the berthing arrangements on piles within the harbour.*

YARMOUTH HARBOUR

Plan No. 20

High Water (*Mean*) — o *h.* 28 *m. Dover.*
Rise 8.4 *ft. springs;* 6.6 *ft. neaps.*
Depths *Tide gauges are placed on the pier facing north for incoming vessels and on the dolphin facing south for vessels leaving the harbour. There is* 5½ *ft. in the entrance at M.L.W.S., and from* 1½ *to* 2 *fathoms within the harbour itself.*

YARMOUTH provides a good protected harbour available to yachts at all states of the tide. The town itself is a beautiful one, especially when viewed from seaward. It provides the most convenient and popular port in the Solent.

Approach and Entrance Yarmouth can be located from a considerable distance by its conspicuous pier. There is plenty of water in the approaches from east or west off the pierhead, but there is a local tide rip situated near the Black Rock (marked by black conical buoy) about 3 cables westward of the pier. With sufficient rise of tide small craft can pass inside the Black Rock (awash at L.W.) by keeping the end of the pier at Fort Victoria in line with the south side of Hurst Castle. This passage carries 2 ft. M.L.W.S., but do not go north of the line until Black Rock has been passed.

The harbour entrance lies just to the west of the pier, and there are two leading marks on the quay (white diamonds on posts) which indicate the best water in the approach channel. At the entrance there is a large dolphin (used for warping the ferry under bad conditions) close to the end of the breakwater on the starboard hand and the ferry jetty on the port hand. Deeper water will be found by keeping nearer (but not too close) to the jetty but avoid the slipway at its inner end and bear to starboard towards the middle row of piles. The Harbour Master usually gives berthing instructions from the quay, but yachts should have warps and fenders ready for mooring temporarily. The harbour has been dredged to allow for rows of pile moorings, between which are narrow fairways. There is little room for a yacht to tack, and most use auxiliary power, or warp into position. Motor yachts should reduce speed. When the harbour is full a red flag is flown from a flagpole at the seaward end of the ferry jetty at the harbour entrance, or at night two red lights vertical are exhibited from the same point. Yachts may then enter only with permission of the Harbour Master.

Lights There is a fixed red light at the end of the long outer pier. Two fixed green lights are placed on the leading marks on the quay, which lead in at 181°

as far as the ferry jetty. There is a fixed red light at the end of this jetty which is left to port when entering, after which course is gradually altered to starboard. At the far end of the quay there is a fixed white light facing westwards across the harbour but showing red towards the quay itself.

Moorings and Anchorage Yachts berth alongside each other, moored stem and stern to the mooring piles provided for the purpose. The Harbour Master will indicate which berth to take. Each line of piles has a letter and each berth a number. There is no anchorage in the harbour, but above the swing bridge there is room to anchor in the river. Outside there is anchorage to west or east of the end of the pier, although the swell from passing liners causes temporary discomfort, and the anchorage is untenable when it blows strongly from any northerly direction. Bring up a little inside the line of the pier end if draught permits.

Facilities There is a good combined ironmonger's and yacht chandler's, usually open, hotels and several shops. Early closing day, Thursday. Water and petrol may be obtained on the quay. Petrol also from yacht

62.   *Yarmouth looking North out of harbour from slipway, showing dolphin at entrance, old quay and ferry slip.*

chandler. There are small boat builders, and a grid. Launching sites from dinghy slip at the quay or from the ferry slip by arrangement with the Harbour Master; car park adjacent. Yacht club: R. Solent Y.C. Frequent ferry service to Lymington. Buses run to Newport.

63.   *Yarmouth from bridge showing training wall and quay.*

LYMINGTON

Plan No. 21

High Water (*Mean*) — o h. 11 m. *Dover.*
Rise 8.5 *ft. springs;* 6.9 *ft. neaps.*
Depths *About* 8 *ft. at entrance at M.L.W.S. deepening to* 12 *ft. within, then shallowing to about* 6 *ft. There is water for yachts drawing* 7½ *ft. up to the shipyard at about one hour either side of M.L.W.S., and at all hours at neaps.*

LYMINGTON RIVER provides a good harbour available to most yachts at all states of the tide. It is a pleasant place in which to bring up. Lymington itself is a small and rather charming Hampshire town, which provides yachtsmen with all facilities.

Approach and Entrance The entrance lies about ¾ mile north-west of Lymington Spit buoy. The Lymington Yacht Club building is conspicuous from seaward, and the river pursues a winding channel between the mud flats towards it. The channel is marked at the entrance by Jack in the Basket (beacon with barrel top and black disc) on the south-west. On the other side to the north-east, is a diamond-topped beacon and the racing staging of the yacht club. The river is clearly marked. On the port side the posts have black discs at the top and on the starboard white triangles. The best water is on the west side of the channel.

Lights Two red leading lights on pylons near the Royal Lymington Yacht Club give the channel over the bar and up Long Reach at 320°. These should not be followed above Semour's Post where the river bends to the north. There are lights on posts to mark the channel which are exhibited all the year round. They consist of an isophase and three red flashing lights on the west (port) side and an isophase and three white flashing on the east (starboard) side.

Anchorage Anchorage is now prohibited in the river, which is fully occupied by private moorings. These should not be picked up without permission. Arrangements for berthing, particularly for large yachts, may be made with the Harbour Master. The following are the principal positions: (1) On mooring piles below the bridge, where there is about 3½ ft. M.L.W.S., but a soft bottom so that the keel sinks into the mud and yachts remain upright at low water. (2) Alongside Custom House quay, 170 ft. long, up to about six abreast. About 3 ft. M.L.W.S. alongside to 6 ft. some 20 ft. from the quay, i.e., third berth out. (3) Apply at Berthon Boat Co. Ltd. Marina, where there are 140 excellent berths, some of which are available to visitors by arrangement. (4) Lymington Yacht Haven, new marina (1969) Harper's Lake.

65. *Jack in the Basket beacon at entrance on the port hand.*

64. *Lymington River. The picture faces down river towards Solent. [Photo: Aero Pictorial]*

66. *Lymington Y.C. staging for starting box on the starboard hand near the entrance.*

Facilities Water at the Shipyard or at Town Quay or Marinas. Petrol at Shipyard or Marinas. Shops of all kinds and hotels. Early closing Wednesday. First-class yacht building and repairing of all kinds at Shipyard. Also other yacht yards. Stations at Lymington pier on east side of river and at Lymington Town close to the Town Quay. Electric service, London 1¾ hrs. Bus service to local districts. Southampton and Bournemouth. Launching sites at public slipway adjacent yacht club, or at slipway at Town Quay. Car parks near. Yacht clubs: R. Lymington Y.C., Lymington Town S.C.

67.   *Lymington Yacht Club* (conspicuous from seaward) *and ferry passing.*

KEYHAVEN

Plan No. 22

High Water (*Mean*) — o h. 28 m. *Dover*.
Rise 8½ *ft. springs; 7 ft. neaps.*
Depths *On the bar there is about 2 ft. M.L.W.S. For*

¼ *mile within the entrance there are between 2 or 3 fathoms, and there is a fathom for ¼ mile above the entrance of Mount Lake after which the channel shallows.*

THE ENTRANCE to Keyhaven is exposed to easterly winds, but in normal conditions the river makes a very pleasant harbour for small craft. Unfortunately, nowa-

68.   *Hurst Narrows looking north across channel. Fort Albert on right and position of Keyhaven indicated by yachts off the entrance.*

days it is very crowded with moorings and it is difficult to find room to anchor. The bar makes the entrance rather inconvenient from the east, as if a yacht comes down on the last of the ebb she will have a longish wait for sufficient water to enter. If bound east from Keyhaven there is a similar wait for sufficient water over the bar.

Approach and Entrance Keyhaven lies on the north side of the Solent, just within Hurst Point. In crossing the Solent allow for the very strong tides.

Shape a course for a position about $\frac{1}{4}$ mile north-eastward of the old pier near Hurst High light. The channel entrance will then be seen, just eastward of the northern spit of the long shingle bank which runs from Hurst Castle northwards so far as Keyhaven River. This shingle bank extends eastwards and dries out 4 ft. M.L.W.S., for about a cable seawards, so the line of the shore cannot be followed up closely. The best approach is from the direction of Yarmouth to the north spit of the shingle bank. Steer for the spit and round it closely on the south side of the river, keeping well clear of the shoal on the north side where there are occasional perches to mark it. Then follow the direction of the channel as shown by the moored boats.

The leading marks for the approach are not very clear. In 1967 the outer post had a rectangular black board to be brought into line with the distant (and lower) mark which was a red can on a post. These marks are not so important as they used to be as there is no longer a channel across the bar, where the depths are now fairly uniform. All that is necessary is to steer for the shingle spit on a bearing of about W by N. Within the river the perches on the starboard hand have triangle topmarks and those to port X topmarks but they are often in delapidated condition.

In the Camber on the south side of the channel there are two shallow creeks leading up towards Hurst Castle, and $\frac{1}{2}$ mile within the entrance the main channel is joined by a creek named Mount Lake which runs westward. There are no lights in Keyhaven Lake.

Anchorage The best positions in Keyhaven are occupied by moorings. Strangers will have to anchor nearer the entrance or make enquiries to ascertain whether a mooring is available. Buoy the anchor, as telegraph cables are laid along the west side of the channel and twice between Hurst Castle and Mount Lake. *Outside*. With moderate westerly winds there is an anchorage off the mud flats, and also holding ground close to the old pier, near Hurst High light in 2 fathoms. Strong tide here.

Facilities There is a general stores, inn and post office at Keyhaven. Early closing day, Wednesday. Water at boat yard or by permission from club. At Milford-on-Sea, distant 1 mile, there are good shopping facilities, hotel and garage with petrol. Early closing,

Wednesday. At Keyhaven yachts can be scrubbed on the hard where there is 6 ft. of water at high spring tides. There is a boat yard. Launching site at hard near club, with car park adjacent. Yacht clubs: Keyhaven Y.C., Hurst Castle S.C. Bus service to Lymington.

69. *Keyhaven—yacht club and hard.*

CHRISTCHURCH

Plan No. 23

High Water (*Harbour*) (*Mean*) — 0 h. 26 m. *Dover. High water is over an hour earlier at spring tides and an hour later at neaps.*

Rise (*Harbour*) *4.9 ft. springs; 4.1 ft. neaps.*

Depths *About 1½ ft. M.L.W.S., and 7 ft. maximum high water on bar. Off Mudeford Quay there is over 7 ft. M.L.W.S. In the channel up to Christchurch there is considerable variation in depth—from 3 to 10 ft.*

OWING to the shallow water over the bar 4 ft. is the maximum draft for entry at H.W., except on exceptionally high tides, and with local knowledge. But once the difficulties of the entrance have been overcome, Christchurch harbour will be found an interesting place to visit. At Mudeford there is good bathing, and Christchurch itself is a beautiful old town, famous for the priory.

Approach and Entrance The entrance to Christchurch lies about a mile north of the conspicuous Hengistbury Head—see Passage Notes—and ½ mile S.W. of a conspicuous white dome on the Avon beach. The bar shifts frequently and varies in depth. Onshore winds and heavy swells make the entrance dangerous,

70. *Christchurch entrance looking south-west along the run as seen when entering harbour. Haven House and quay on right—Hengistbury Head centre distance—Black House and some of the beach huts to left.*

but in westerly winds some shelter is provided by Hengistbury Head which protects the entrance from the west.

There are two dangers when approaching from the west. Firstly the Christchurch ledges and secondly the Clarendon rocks off the shore on the south side of the entrance. From the north-east there are no outlying dangers, but on nearer approach frequent soundings should be taken to ensure an adequate depth of water.

Numbers of bathing huts and a black house on sand dunes will be seen south of the entrance. The Haven House, which is on the north side of the river near the entrance, should be identified, but the position of entrance varies. In 1967 the entrance was 2½ cables north-east of Haven House, and the channel across the bar marked on the port hand by four red and white can buoys, and to starboard by three black spherical buoys. These are placed in position during the summer months by the Christchurch Harbour Association, but they occasionally drag in bad weather. The inside channel, which lies parallel with the shore, is known as the 'Run'. The Run is very narrow and on the ebb the tide is a veritable torrent.

71. *Christchurch entrance—looking west across 'The Run' to the end of Haven Quay and Haven House on extreme right (half cut off).*

The middle of Christchurch harbour, like Teignmouth is choked with an expanse of mud, leaving a shallow gully, leading northward, but the main channel is to the southward. After several turns it leads to Christchurch; it is marked by buoys and has depths ranging from 3 to 5 ft., with deeper pools.

Moorings and Anchorages (1) Outside, good holding ground off the entrance in offshore winds. (2) Do *not* anchor in the Run as the ebb is too strong, but anchor beyond the Haven House in the reach running S.S.W., in 5 to 6 ft. There are many private moorings here now. (3) At south end of Steep Bank (the reach south-east of the quay) in 9 ft.; only a short row by dinghy to quay. (4) Elsewhere in the harbour as convenient. (5) Moorings are often available in the first S.S.W. reach, or near the yacht club, where there is a visitor's mooring, or on application to Elkin's yacht yard.

Facilities Water at Haven House, and town quay, Christchurch. Petrol and oil at quayside and boat yards. Stores, post office and yacht yard at Christchurch. Early closing day, Wednesday. Also stores and water can be obtained from the cafe near the concrete jetty at Mudeford spit. Launching sites: (1) Slipway at Christchurch quay. (2) At yacht club, by permission. (3) At Elkin's yacht yard. (4) From beach on harbour side of Haven quay. Car parks adjacent. Four yacht or boat yards. Yacht club: Christchurch S.C. Frequent buses and trains from Christchurch.

72. *Christchurch—the quay and yacht club, close up.*

POOLE

Plan No. 24a and 24b

High Water *At entrance: (mean)* — o h. 36 m. *Dover. High water is nearly 2 hours earlier at spring tides and nearly an hour later at neaps.*

Rise (*Entrance*) 5.6 ft. springs; 4.3 ft. neaps.

Depths 10½ ft. M.L.W.S. on bar; deepens in the 'Swash' channel and the main channel; 12 ft. M.L.W.S. in 'Stakes' channel to Poole town and at quayside.

POOLE HARBOUR is nearly 100 miles in circumference and the numerous channels provide interesting pilotage for small yachts. There are several privately-owned small islands, and in the centre is the comparatively large Brownsea Island, now owned by the National Trust and well worth a visit. There is plenty of water for yachts of average size in the main channels, which are clearly marked, but the upper reaches of the various branches are uneven in depth and mostly shallow.

Double high water lasts for over 3 hrs., but rise and fall of tide is much affected by wind conditions.

Approach and entrance The prominent feature in the approach to Poole is the chalk Handfast Point, with Old Harry rocks off it. The bar buoy is situated a mile N.N.E. of Handfast Point, and about 2 miles beyond the buoy will be seen the harbour entrance, with the conspicuous Haven Hotel on the east side.

There is an ugly sea on the bar and in the Swash entrance channel during strong south to east winds, particularly on the ebb, when the approach may be dangerous. On the ebb there is a tide rip off Handfast Point, and the tide runs fiercely out of the narrow entrance between the Haven Points.

The entrance channel named the Swash runs in at 324° true (N.W. by N.¾N. mag.) between sands and a training bank on the west side, and the Hook sand on the east side. The outer buoy is the conical Bar light buoy and the channel is buoyed with red and white can and barrel buoys (P) and black conical buoys (S), but the unlit buoys are close on the edge of the channel. There is a dolphin at the end of the training bank. At the Channel Light buoy (near the inner end of the training bank) alter course to 316° true (N.W. by N. mag.) and steer for the entrance leaving to starboard the Haven Hotel. A chain ferry crosses the entrance here.

Inside the entrance the channel divides into two. One part (South Deep) runs south-west whilst the main channel swings around between Sandbanks and Brownsea Island in a north-easterly direction and leads to Poole.

The Harbour The main channel bears to N.N.E.

73. *Harbour entrance at Sandbanks showing chain ferry approaching hard at Sandbanks. Brownsea Island in background. The conspicuous Haven Hotel is out of the picture to the right.*

74. *Within the entrance at sandbanks looking north to Brownsea Castle and island. Power station chimneys on right.*

off North Haven Point and the Middle Ground spherical R.W.H.S. light buoy is left to port. The channel is well marked by R.W. can buoys with even numbers to port and black conical buoys to starboard. The port hand buoys should not be passed closely. At Salterns pier the channel is narrow and the beacon should be left close to starboard. On arrival off Poole enter the Little or Stakes channel leaving No. 42 R.W. barrel buoy to port and black conical Stakes buoy to starboard. Then leave the Hamworthy quay to port and two posts on the mud and buoy to starboard before altering course again to enter Poole town harbour.

The Wych channel is to the west of the Main channel leaving the Middle Ground spherical buoy to starboard. It leads on the east side of Brownsea Island and then along the mud flats on the north side and southwards along the west side, finally pursuing a wandering course between the mud flats to Shipstal Point and then southwards. It is deep and marked on each side by occasional piles on the mud but shoals west of Brownsea Island.

The Diver channel (6 ft. least water) lies between the Main channel and the Wych channel. It is the shortest way to Poole, but not easy to strangers. Leave the Middle Ground buoy to starboard and steer for Salterns pier true north. Leave Aunt Betty buoy (R.W.V.S.) No. 54 close to port. Alter course to port to 297°. The channel is then marked by stakes on each side, those on the port hand having can topmarks, and it joins the Main channel at the conical black Diver buoy which is left to starboard. Shallow draft vessels where possible should keep clear of ships confined to deep channels.

South Deep branches off to the south-west, west of North Haven Point and is entered between No. 50A barrel buoy B.W. to starboard and No. 18 R.W. buoy to port, but do not round the port hand buoy sharply as there is a gravel bank in the vicinity. Steer south-west until the stakes are located—black to starboard, red to port. South Deep is not difficult to follow and it is deep as far as and $\frac{1}{4}$ mile beyond Goathorn Point. The channel lies between mud flats with beautiful heath land and distant hills to the south. There are no lights.

The upper reaches of the various channels are marked by stakes and are navigable, but great care is required in keel yachts as the bottom is very uneven. They are ideal for centreboard and light draft yachts.

Lights By night the approach is easy. Sail from Poole Bar buoy (Fl. 5 sec.) to the Channel buoy (Fl. R. 5 sec.) leaving the training bank dolphin (Fl. R. 5 sec.) to port. Then sail up the entrance towards Brownsea buoy (Fl. R. 10 sec.) passing between the ferry hards (2 F.R. to starboard and 2 Fl. R. 4 sec. to port) Leave to starboard North Haven dolphin (Fl. 5 sec.). Altering course here, proceed up the main chan-

75. *Little or Stakes channel leading to Poole quay.* [*Photo: Aero Films Ltd.*]

nel between red flashing buoys to port and white flashing buoys to starboard. Salterns pier beacon (Gp. Fl. 3, 10 sec.) is left close to starboard.

Anchorages (1) Outside. There is excellent holding ground in Studland Bay, protected from westerly and south-westerly winds. Small village with hotels, post office and grocer about ¼ mile inshore. Early closing Thursday. (2) Off Brownsea Island, but most of the area is occupied by moorings. Hail the R.M.Y.C. launchman for advice or enquire at the R.M.Y.C. (who make visiting yachtsmen welcome) or at one of the yacht yards. (3) Moorings may sometimes be had inside the entrance on the east side in North Haven Lake, off the yacht yard. Apply to boatman, yacht yard or yacht club. (4) Alongside the quay in Poole town on north side, west of Harbour Master's office. (5) Above Poole off Dorset Yacht Co., Hamworthy, where there are usually moorings for hire, and attendance. (6) In west arm of harbour, i.e. in South Deep, as far up as Goathorn Point.

Anchorage may be found anywhere in Poole harbour by choosing a position protected by land from the wind and free from moorings which are laid in all the best spots. In strong winds anchorage in the main channels may be uncomfortable for small boats, but shelter may be found in Poole town, or under a weather shore such as the Wych channel (protected from south by Brownsea Island) or off Goathorn Point (protection from south-west).

Facilities Water at tap or by hose on application at Harbour Master's office at Poole. Petrol at garage at bridge or at yacht yards or at quay by arrangement. Refueller moored in Diver Channel west of Aunt Betty buoy. Ship chandlers. Yacht brokers. Sailmakers. Hotel and many shops. Early closing Wednesday. Yacht yards at Sandbanks, Parkstone and Hamworthy. Launching sites: Lilliput Yacht Service, Sandbanks Rd. End of quay farthest from Poole bridge or by arrangement with yacht yards. Yacht clubs: Lilliput S.C., R. Motor Y.C., Parkstone Y.C., Poole Harbour Y.C., Poole Y.C., Wareham S.C., Redcliffe S.C., East Dorset S.C., Converted Cruiser Club.

SWANAGE

IN SETTLED weather in westerly winds between N.W. and south-west there is a pleasant anchorage off the pier. When approaching care should be taken to avoid Peveril ledges off the south extremity of Swanage Bay. The tide sets strongly across the ledges, and there is a race off the point.

Small craft usually anchor W by N of the pier in 6 to 8 ft., seaward of local moorings, and larger yachts farther out, but the holding ground is not so good as at Studland Bay, which has the additional advantage of Poole near at hand as a port of refuge in case of a change of wind or weather. There are some visitor's moorings by arrangement with boatmen on the beach.

Excellent hotels and shopping facilities. Early closing Thursday. Good sailing club (Swanage S.C.) which welcomes holiday membership. Launching site at slipway near pier with car park adjacent. Station and buses.

76. *Swanage—Pier on left with sailing club at inner end. Beach for landing on right. Anchor outside local boats and mooring buoys.*

LULWORTH COVE

Plan No. 25

High Water (*Approximate*) —04 h. 00 m. Dover.
Rise 7 *ft. springs;* 4.5 *ft. neaps.*
Depths *About* 16 *ft. in entrance;* 12 *ft. M.L.W.S. in centre, shallows towards shore.*

LULWORTH should only be visited in settled weather and during offshore winds. A shift of wind to south or south-west, bringing with it a strong blow as so frequently happens, will send a heavy swell into the cove. In such conditions power vessels may find it difficult to get out in safety and the task of beating out under sail may prove too dangerous to attempt. Therefore, clear out if the weather threatens to change and if caught inside, apply to local boatmen for heavy anchors and cables.

Lulworth Cove is in a lovely setting and is worth altering course to visit.

Approach and Entrance Lulworth is not always easy to identify from seaward, but the photograph reproduced will help. To the west there runs a series of white cliffs with curved summits. The entrance is just to the east of a sugar-loaf hill with a coastguard hut situated upon it.

There are no outlying dangers except for the gunnery range between Lulworth and St. Albans—see Passage Notes. Steer straight in keeping rather to the east of the centre of the entrance to avoid the rocks off the West Point. Just within the entrance there are rocks to port and starboard of the fairway, which then opens into the wide cove itself.

As may be expected, the wind is fluky or squally at the entrance, and frequently baffling when entering under sail.

Anchorage Let go anchor in about 12 ft., in the N.E. corner of the cove where the holding ground is blue clay. Avoid anchoring in the fairway used by the pleasure steamers which enter and land passengers on the beach on the N.W. side of cove.

Facilities Water at beach café. Petrol and oil at garage. Small hotels. Shops, early closing Wednesday/Saturday. P.O. Boatbuilders. Launching site from beach at end of road, with car park adjacent. Stores at Boon's stores during summer months. Buses run frequently in summer months. Nearest station, Wool, 5 miles distant.

77. *Lulworth Cove showing the cliff formations to the westward towards White Nothe. The excursion steamer indicates the entrance to the cove.* [*Photo: Aero Films*]

78. *Weymouth approach. The small sewer buoy in front of the cranes. The large blue and white light buoy (port hand) is conspicuous in this picture and lies just east of Sewer buoy. The Nothe Fort is on the left.*

79. *Weymouth entrance from sewer buoy.*

WEYMOUTH

Plan No. 26

High Water —04 h. 38 m. Dover.
Rise 7 ft. springs; 4.5 ft. neaps.
Tides *The tides are 4 hrs. flood, 4 hrs. ebb, and 4 slack subject to the 'Gulder' as it is called, which is a small flood making its way into the harbour about ¾ hr. after the first L.W.*
Depths *There is 15 ft. M.L.W.S. in the entrance, and to within a cable of the bridge, when it begins to shallow. On the quayside and jetties on north side there is about 10 to 12 ft. but less on the south side.*

WEYMOUTH, as popular seaside resorts go, is a pleasant one. The town provides all facilities for yachtsmen, and there is a good train service to London via Dorchester, Poole and Southampton. The harbour is sheltered but in strong winds there is often an uncomfortable roll at the visitor's yacht moorings and it is necessary to proceed farther up.

Approach and Entrance The harbour lies about ½ mile north of the Portland harbour breakwaters. The entrance is between two piers. On the south is the Nothe Hill, and on the north pier is the pavilion. The jubilee clock—conspicuous—is about ½ mile east along the front. Approaching from the eastward a series of buoys—see chart—will be left to port. Two of these are light buoys, the outer Bl. W. (Fl. 5 sec.)

80. *The Nothe and yacht moorings on right. Photograph taken from end of south breakwater.*

81. *The north pier and Pavilion.*

and the inner B.Y. (Fl. R.) which lies off the Mixen rocks and sewer outfall. Then steer a cable off the entrance and round in between the two piers. Keep a look out for hauling-off lines across the harbour when a Channel Island steamer is about to depart.

Anchorage Visiting yachts during daylight will usually be directed to a berth by the Pier Master. (1) Moored fore and aft alongside other yachts to buoys on the south side of harbour under the Nothe. (2) If there is a swell go right up the harbour and moor alongside the quay on the port side about 100 yds. short of the bridge. This is the most popular berth for small yachts and there is no motion such as there is on the buoys near the entrance. *Outside* In settled weather anchor in $1\frac{1}{2}$ to 2 fathoms about a cable off the north pier, clear of the entrance. Take soundings to find right depth, as shallow water extends a long way seaward.

Lights and Fog Signal North pier, fixed green. South pier, Qk. Fl. (obscured over Mixen rocks). Two fixed R. leading lights on Ballast quay in line at 238° lead in, open of the south pier light. Fog signals when vessels expected. South pier explosives (3) Reed ev. 15 sec. North pier, bell.

Facilities Water at Nothe Walk and at quays. Petrol and oil at quayside of inner harbour. Hotels, restaurants and shops. Early closing Wednesday. Boat builders and repairers. Launching site: from beach, adjacent promenade or at yards. Yacht clubs: R.

82.   *The inner harbour showing Town Bridge. Yachts lie afloat alongside on left in the 'Cove' in positions according to draft.*

Dorset Y.C., Weymouth S.C. Station. Buses.

Regulating Signals A *red flag* over a *green* by day, or *two red* lights over a *green* at night indicate entry or departure forbidden. *Two red* flags by day or *three red* lights by night indicate a vessel is leaving and no vessel shall approach or obstruct the entrance. *Two green* flags by day or *three green* lights by night indicate that a vessel is approaching entrance from seaward and no vessel may leave. *When no signal is shown the entrance is clear both inwards and outwards.*

PORTLAND

Plan No. 27

High Water —04 h. 38 m. Dover.
Rise 7 ft. springs; 4.5 ft. neaps.

PORTLAND HARBOUR lies in the bay formed by the mainland on the north, the long narrow strip of the Chesil beach on the west, and the high peninsula of Portland on the south. From the east it is protected by three big breakwaters which create a very large artificial harbour. This is primarily a naval base but it also provides a shelter for yachts, though the anchorages are limited.

Strangers should remember that it is a naval port. Within the harbour there are numerous unlit floating targets, mooring buoys, etc., and cables on bottom. Attention is also drawn to the increasing number of naval exercises being carried out from Portland and in the adjacent waters with both submarine and surface craft. Also at night exercises often involve flares, Very lights and flashes, etc.

Approach and Entrance Portland is so conspicuous that it is easy to identify. It is a high peninsula that, viewed from seaward, resembles an island, but the highest part is at the northern end, and the southern extremity (the Bill) is low. See Passage Notes.

The principal danger to navigation in the approach to Portland is the Race. This is the most dangerous disturbance on the whole of the south coast, and the time of tide has to be studied—see Passage Notes. Other dangers in the area are: (a) In and around the mining area to the West of Portland Bill there are unlit buoys in undefined positions used for naval exercises. Position shown on Chart No. 2615. (b) The gunnery range between St. Albans Hd. and Lulworth—see Passage Notes.

The harbour itself may be located behind its long stone breakwaters, northward of the heights of Portland. There were three entrances, but the South Ship channel has been closed. The two entrances in use are the middle and northern ones.

Principal Lights and Fog Signals Portland Bill lighthouse: Gp. Fl. ev. 20 sec. 18 M. Gradually changes 1 Fl. to 4 Fl. from 221° to 244°, 4 Fl. thence to 117°, gradually changes to 1 Fl. thence to 141° obscured elsewhere. Fixed red light below visible over Shambles 271° to 291°. Diaphone 30 sec. Shambles L.V.: Gp. Fl. (2) 30 sec., 11 M. Diaphone (2) 60 sec. South-west end of outer breakwater: Occ. R. ev. 30 sec. 5 M. obscured seaward. East Ship channel: (N) Fl. ev. 10 sec. 14 M.; (S) Fixed R. 2 M. Keep sharp look out for weak red light inconspicuous compared with white. North

83. *Castle Cove from south-west showing sailing club high up in trees and club jetty at low water.*

84. *Portland harbour. Castletown beach, the only public landing place on the south side of the harbour other than at the Naval Centre pontoons.*

85. *Portland harbour. Castletown looking east across the harbour to the naval dockyard.*

86. *Portland Bill. Close up from the west looking east. Showing lighthouse signal staff (for gale warnings etc.) and daymark right on the end.*

Ship channel: (N) Occ. ev. 10 sec., 5 M.; (S) Occ. R. 15 sec., 5 M.

Regulations The following are some of the most important of the naval regulations for Portland, where all ships are under direction of Q.H.M. Keep clear of H.M. vessels with 'M' flag over Pilot Jack, or red light on foremost head, denoting she is underway to enter or leave the harbour. Signals from E. Weare Signal Station; red oblong flag with white diagonal bar on northern arm of flagstaff (or one white over two red lights) prohibits entry by North Ship channel. The same flag on southern arm of flagstaff (or two red over one white light) prohibit entry by East Ship channel. Flag at masthead (or three red lights vertical) prohibit entry by either channel. In bad visibility signals given from 'A' head on north side of East Ship channel.

Anchorage There is anchorage off Old Castle Cove in the north-west of the harbour, with depths of 1 or 2 fathoms. Yachts should anchor as close in as possible, though the best positions are occupied by private yacht moorings. It is better to endeavour to get use of a vacant mooring by applying first to the boatman or the Castle Cove S.C. Visiting yachtsmen are usually permitted to use the landing-stage belonging to the sailing club. There is water from a tap on the shore. Post office, shops and town are ¼ mile away. To Weymouth is a walk of over ½ mile, or alternatively go by bus.

In strong southerly winds this anchorage is too exposed. In this case bring uo in 8 to 10 ft., clay bottom, off Castletown. Moorings are sometimes available here, or there is anchorage to the west of the R.3. Hard, ½ mile west of Castletown. Yachtsmen are allowed to land on the Naval Sailing Centre pontoons close to the castle. No public landing except on the beach. Castletown pier is private, and the landing steps are usually locked by a gate. Also note that only H.M. ships are permitted to anchor east of a line running north near Quebec pier and defined by two white obelisks ashore.

Facilities at Castletown. Water from hotel or public house. Petrol from garage. Post office and shops. Early closing Wednesday. Yacht yards at ferry bridge. Launching site: rather restricted but light boats can be launched from Castletown beach, road adjacent or from beach adjacent to bridge at Wyke Regis which joins mainland to Chesil causeway. Yacht clubs: Castle Cove S.C., Portland Naval S.A.

BRIDPORT

Plan No. 28

High Water −04 h. 53 m. Dover.
Rise 12 ft. springs; 8.4 ft. neaps.

Depths *Bar within entrance between piers practically dries out. From 2 ft. to 5 ft. within harbour, one deep berth, but most parts dry out.*

BRIDPORT suffers from the usual disadvantage of a shallow artificial harbour which has a long narrow entrance. The entrance is dangerous in hard onshore

87.   *Bridport Harbour. [Photo: Aero Films]*

88. *Bridport entrance from south-west showing conspicuous buildings just east of entrance and North Hill on right of photo.*

89. *Bridport entrance from south.*

weather. Once inside the harbour a yacht may be weather bound waiting for fair conditions before attempting to leave, but this old West Country port is worth a visit, and offers a pleasant break to the passage across West Bay. The coaster trade is increasing with the import of timber and export of shingle. Near L.W.

the sluice gates are opened and the entrance is scoured with the water released.

Approach and Entrance The approach to Bridport harbour is simple enough so far as outlying dangers are concerned, but the harbour entrance is unsafe in strong onshore winds, as the sea breaks heavily outside even at high water.

When a vessel is expected and when there is sufficient depth a pilot flag is hoisted on the east pier flagstaff; when the entrance is considered unsafe a black ball is hoisted. The presence of these signals should not be relied upon for yachts, as they are hoisted for ships.

The only outlying shoals are the Pollock ($7\frac{1}{2}$ ft. M.L.W.S.) to the south-west, and the High Ground (9 to 14 ft. M.L.W.S.) to the west. From the west to steer between these shoals bring North Hill on east side of harbour in line with east pier at 75° true. E. $\frac{1}{2}$ N. mag.

From south or east, steer straight off the entrance and enter but beware of the backwash off the piers. The recognized line of approach is west pier and Down Hall (above Bridport town) in line at 011°. The bar lies within the entrance along the line of the foreshore, 10 ft. to 14 ft. at M.H.W.S. The channel is long and narrow (40 ft.) and sailing craft without auxiliaries will need to be towed in during offshore winds.

Lights The entrance should not be attempted by strangers at night. A new light Fl. W. (Occ. $1\frac{1}{2}$ sec.) is established permanently on Harbour Master's office on foreshore just west of west pier, but this serves only as a guide to the position of the harbour. When a vessel is expected weak pilot lights are exhibited: F.G. on east pierhead and F.R. on west pierhead.

Anchorages and Moorings (1) Outside the harbour in settled weather with offshore winds. Anchor in 3 or 4 fathoms abreast the piers about $\frac{1}{4}$ mile off. (2) Inside the harbour consult the Harbour Master. Small yachts dry out at the west end of the harbour, or alongside the harbour walls. There is one deep berth, 12 ft., alongside north end of quay where scour from sluice makes a deep hole. This can be used by permission of Harbour Master when no coaster is expected. Otherwise berth at east end of harbour drying alongside quay, soft mud bottom. If disengaged, moorings may be hired for small yachts in shallow water.

Facilities Water from hydrants near the quay, all stores. Early closing day, Thursday. Scrubbing inside harbour; no yacht yard. Launching site: good slip and adjacent car park. Good bus connexions; railway station 2 miles from harbour.

90. *Lyme Regis approach from south showing beacon and breakwater of Portland stones off the end of the Cobb.*

91. *Entrance of Lyme Regis harbour from the eastward.*

LYME REGIS

High Water —04 *h.* 53 *m. Dover.*
Rise 12.3 *ft. springs;* 8.6 *ft. neaps.*
Depths 6 *to* 12 *ft. about 2 cables east of the entrance. Harbour dries out at L.W. and entrance is shallow.*

LYME REGIS and its harbour are picturesque and worth visiting, though crowded in the holiday season. The harbour dries out but a berth alongside the quay is sheltered from northerly, westerly and south-west winds and under these conditions the harbour is said to be safe even in gales. In strong onshore winds the approach is rough and in south-east gales the entrance is dangerous and the swell enters the harbour.

Approach and Entrance Lyme Regis is just east of the centre of Lyme Bay, some 22 miles west of Portland Bill. The approach is straightforward. The harbour is protected from the west by the long stone pier known as 'The Cobb', which is forked at its eastern end. Off the outer fork is a beacon marking a heap of large Portland stones, serving as a breakwater and covered at half flood. There are also stones and rocks all along the west and south of the Cobb.

The entrance to the harbour lies between the eastern end of the inner fork of the Cobb and the southern end of the detached breakwater which affords partial protection to the harbour from the east. The entrance is narrow.

Steer for the beacon off the outer fork of the Cobb, leaving it about 50 yds. to port and hold on until the harbour entrance is opened up. Then steer in, with sufficient rise of tide, to enter the harbour. Depth gauge in entrance on north wall.

Leading Lights Front light on inner pierhead fixed W.R. 2 M. Rear light on old Custom House fixed R. 2 M. Lights in line lead in at 296°. The lights are weak and on approach are rendered inconspicuous by the many town lights ashore.

Anchorages and Moorings (1) Anchor outside the harbour in settled weather in offshore winds to the east of the entrance in about 12 ft. With the aid of careful soundings it is possible to find 8 ft. further north but the bottom shoals rapidly towards the shore. There is swell in anchorage if wind east or if there is any south in the wind. (2) The harbour dries out and yachtsmen either moor in the middle of the harbour on hard bottom if able to take the ground, or berth alongside quay. A berth is reserved for visiting yachts alongside quay opposite sailing club. Depths in harbour 9 to 14 ft. at M.H.W.S. Clean sand bottom alongside the quay.

Facilities Water at shoreward end of the Cobb.

Petrol and oil on parade. Hotels and shops. Early closing Thursday. Scrubbing can be arranged and small yacht repairs. Launching site, slip and car park adjacent. Dinghy park. Buses to all parts and railway station ½ mile from harbour. Yacht club: Lyme Regis S.C.

BEER

IN NORTHERLY winds and settled weather there is a delightful anchorage for small yachts off Beer. This is sheltered from the north through west by Beer Head. Beer Head (see Passage Notes) is a precipitous headland, 426 ft. high, and easy to identify, as it is the most westerly chalk cliff in England. The anchorage is on the west side of the small bay east of Beer Head, as close to the shore as soundings show desirable. Approaching from the westward, round Beer Head and

92. *Lyme Regis harbour. [Photo: Aero Films]*

93. *Rounding Beer Head from the westward.*

follow up the cliffs (which have rocks at their base) keeping on the west side towards the conspicuous road which leads from the shore to the village and church. Approaching from the eastward give a wide berth to the headland on the east side of the cove, which has rocks extending over a cable off it, before turning into the anchorage. Land by dinghy on beach which is steep. There are local fishermen and boatmen who will ferry to the yacht or attend to the dinghy.

With any forecast of change in wind leave quickly. The local fishing boats are hauled up on the beach out of danger. For yachts the nearest good harbour of refuge is Brixham.

Facilities Hotels, shops. Early closing Thursday. Boatbuilder. Launching site from the road leading down to the beach which is steep and suitable for launching.

94. *Beer Bay and anchorage.*

EXMOUTH

High Water —04 h. 53 m. *Dover. At Topsham* ½ *h. later.*

Rise (*at entrance*) 12.4 *ft. springs;* 8.7 *ft. neaps.*

Depths *There may be* 4 *ft. or less in parts on the bar; after which the channel deepens. Within the harbour the bottom is uneven. There are deep stretches with over* 5 *fathoms in parts off Exmouth town and off the Warren, but most of the channel as far as Starcross is from* 16 *to* 4 *ft. and the channel tends to shoal towards Topsham and practically dries out in the upper reaches.*

THE RIVER EXE provides some 6 miles of navigable channel. It is worth visiting when cruising in the West Country. The only harbour is a small tidal dock at Exmouth town but there are several anchorages. It should not be regarded as a port of refuge as the sands on the bar are liable to shift and there is a dangerous sea during strong onshore winds, especially with the ebb running against the wind. Under average conditions, however, the approach and entrance is not difficult as it is well buoyed.

Approach and Entrance The outer fairway buoy (spherical bell buoy R.W. vertical bands) is situated ½ mile south-west of Straight Point, which is a low promontory backed by red cliffs, but should not be confused with the lower Orcombe Point a mile westward. There are high cliffs between the two with ledges of rock at their foot. Whatever the direction of the approach, make for the Fairway buoy but when coming from the direction of Torbay or Teignmouth give a good offing to the Pole sands on the south side of the entrance. These are extending eastwards within a ¼ mile of the fairway buoy.

As stated, the entrance should not be attempted during strong onshore winds especially if the ebb has started to run. The easiest time to approach is half flood. This coincides with the turn of the offshore stream to the west. The tidal streams in the offing are weak but are very strong in the entrance and the channel. The sands are liable to shift after gales and the channel between the sands on the port hand and the various ledges and rocks off the coast on the starboard hand is tortuous. It is necessary from the Fairway buoy to steer to the first pair of buoys to the south-east of Orcombe Point and then carefully keep to the channel leaving the even-numbered R. and R.W. can buoys to port and the odd-numbered black conical buoys to starboard. Some of the port hand buoys are very close to the Pole sands so they should not be approached too closely as the sands tend to bulge towards the channel

95. *Entrance to Exmouth facing north-west, with the Fairway buoy to right.*

96. *View from No. 7 buoy heading seawards approximately east-south-east, with Orcombe Point in centre and Straight Point beyond it.*

on the port hand. The streams run like torrents after the last port buoy (No. 10) has been passed and it is best then to keep on the starboard side of the fairway.

The River Off Exmouth the river takes a sharp turn to the south-west between Bull Hill bank in the middle of the harbour and the Warren sands which form a continuation of the Warren (the low point on the south side of the entrance). The main flood sweeps past Exmouth in a north-westerly direction and accordingly course should be altered sharply to port well before reaching the dock in order to get into the stream between Bull Hill bank and the Warren sand and in particular to avoid the shoals extending easterly from Bull Hill bank. The reach of the river south of the Bull Hill bank is called the Bight and it is clearly marked by starboard hand buoys and by mooring buoys on the port hand. The channel follows round Bull Hill bank northward and bends, leaving the Shaggles sand and the spit conical black buoy (which is a starboard hand mark for the Starcross channel) to port. No. 17 starboard hand buoy should be passed closely. Course should then be towards the Limpstone Church to the N.N.E. until the next port hand R.W. buoy (No. 12) has been passed. Having passed No. 12 buoy gradually alter course to port to leave the spit of Limpstone sands to starboard and the three conical starboard buoys No. 21, No. 23 and No. 25. This brings the vessel to Powderham above which follow the buoys

in a shoaling channel with depths as low as 5 ft. as far as Turf Lock. Above Turf Lock the channel is marked by beacons on either side as far as Topsham.

The Starcross channel lies west of the Shaggles sand and carries 4 to 9 ft. of water. It is entered at the spit conical black buoy and although it is unmarked except by a beacon on the port side, the best water can be located by the yachts lying on moorings in it.

When proceeding from Exmouth up the river a considerable saving of distance can be made by passing through the Shelly Gut. This is a shallow channel on the east side of Bull Hill bank but it can only be used with local knowledge as the sands are steep-to on either side and the channel is intricate.

The Western Way This is a swash-way between the Pole sand on the eastward side and the Warren sand on the western side. It has altered and tended to silt up of recent years and requires local knowledge and a shallow draft boat.

Lights It is dangerous for strangers to attempt entrance at night, as the channel is so tortuous that it is impossible to erect leading lights to provide a direct approach. The existing leading lights are placed solely for the assistance of local pilots and navigators and do not lead fairly through the channel.

Straight Point Light F. ev. 10 sec. W.R. 9 M. and 7 M. White 246° to 012½°; red to 022½°; white to 071°.

97.   *View after passing No. 10 buoy and heading towards Exmouth dock with the town on right.*

98.   *Entrance to Exmouth dock at slack water. The tidal streams across the entrance are violent.*

Outer Leading Lights Front fixed W.R. red from 228° to 318°; white thence to 048°. Rear fixed red. The lights in line at 308° lead between the buoys off Orcombe Point.

Inner Leading Lights Situated west end of promenade and at Customs House. Both fixed orange. Leading line 305°. Lead from No. 6 port hand buoy to Checkstone port buoy No. 10, subject to alterations in position of sands and channel. The lights may be altered.

Anchorage and Moorings (1) Temporary anchorage outside off the entrance west of the Fairway buoy in calm weather. (2) Exmouth dock. This is approached through a narrow entrance where ferries berth, and is spanned by a narrow bridge which has to be opened by arrangement with the Harbour Master. The basin is tidal and the north-west side dries out and is occupied by boats. Harbour Master's office is on south side of the bridge and with his permission yachts berth at the south-east quays if these are not occupied by coasters. Depths about 4 ft. M.L.W.S. alongside quay but less water in centre. Keel yachts will partially dry and there are a few ladders. Allow for the fierce tides setting across the entrance. (3) Anchor beyond the entrance to the dock off the Point in 10 ft. clear of the lifeboat. Five-knot tidal stream considered dangerous especially at spring tides or with south-east wind against stream. Stream too fast for rowing dinghy.

(4) Large yachts may anchor in the Bight between Bull Hill bank and Warren sands. (5) West of Bull Hill bank. (6) Off Starcross, south of the pier in 6 to 9 ft. Best positions occupied by moorings. Well sheltered from west. Water and facilities. Early closing day Thursday. Ferry to Exmouth. Main line station. (7) Small craft can anchor in the pool off Powderham in 4 to 5 ft. or in the reach below, clear of the fairway which is used by coasters. (8) Small craft can anchor in 5 ft. south of the landing stage at Turf, clear of the fairway of coasters using the canals, or north of No. 25 buoy.

Exeter Canal The canal is 5 miles long and is entered at Turf Lock. Least depth 11 ft. Locked basin at Exeter.

Facilities at Exmouth. Water by hose at dock. Petrol and oil. Hotels and shops. Early closing day Wednesday. Boatbuilders and repairers. Launching sites: (1) Ramp south of harbour entrance near high water, where yacht club puts a wooden ramp over the soft sand in summer months, little room in road for cars and trailers but car park on the pier. (2) Beach north of harbour entrance. (3) At Limpstone, 2 miles north of Exmouth ramp for launching near H.W. Yacht clubs: Exe S.C., Starcross Y.C., Topsham S.C., Limpstone S.C. Station and bus services.

TEIGNMOUTH

Plan No. 31

High Water −05 *h.* 11 *m. Dover.*
Rise 13.1 *ft. springs;* 9.5 *ft. neaps.*
Depths *About* 1 *ft. to* 2 *ft. M.L.W.S. on the bar; deep pool off Ferry Point, then the depths vary from* 16 *to* 7 *ft. up to Shaldon bridge.*

TEIGNMOUTH is an attractive little seaside town. The harbour on its west and south-west side is well sheltered but the streams are fast so that it is best to hire moorings in preference to anchoring. The entrance is difficult for strangers and the bar makes it dangerous during onshore winds and when a swell is running, as sometimes occurs in advance of a southerly gale.

Approach and Entrance The entrance to the River Teign lies to the northward of the Ness, which is a bold red sandstone headland with pines at its summit which is easy to identify. The Ness and the Pole sand projecting eastward from it flank the south side of the river entrance, and the Spratt sands lie on the north side. Drying sands or shoals extend almost

99. *The Ness (red sandstone) and to right the beacon which may be steered for about* 260° *to* 255°, *skirting the north side of the Pole sand.*

as far as Teignmouth pier, 4 cables to the north-east. The sands on the bar are constantly shifting and in some years steep sandbanks build up. Without a pilot or assistance from local fishermen or boat-owners the entrance should not be attempted by strangers, except with the utmost care in settled weather during offshore winds and on the last quarter of the flood. The following sailing directions form a rough guide to the entrance but should not be relied upon as there are no clear leading marks owing to the shifting sands.

Approach from the southward with the inner end of the pier bearing about north magnetic. When the Ness comes abeam a small black buoy, maintained by the pilots, will be seen. This is usually moored on the west side of the East Pole sand and is left close on the starboard hand. Here there is usually about 1 ft. to 2 ft. M.L.W.S., but the sands alter year by year.

To the west will be seen a white beacon on the north side of the Ness, which stands on a training wall which is covered before half flood. When this beacon bears 260° to 255° steer about 50 yds. off it, taking soundings to skirt the north side of the Pole Sand. On arrival off this beacon steer by chart round the black starboard hand buoy off Ferry Point on the north side of the channel. Note that the sands have crept southwards from the point so the buoy should not be approached too closely. Here the stream runs very hard. Once past Ferry Point alter course quickly to N.E. by N. and steer

for the New Quay leaving a red can buoy well to port. The whole of the centre of the harbour is occupied by the 'Salty Flat' and the river runs on the east of this. Pilotage is easier because the flats are marked by port hand cask buoys. To starboard the shore is fairly steep. After passing the third red port hand buoy keep on the starboard side of the channel on the line of the quays until rounding into the straight reach leading to the bridge. Here the direction of the channel can be judged by mooring buoys.

Lights Strangers should not attempt the entrance

100. *Teignmouth front bearing to the north-west. The swell is breaking on the steep East Pole sand. Ferry Point is out of the picture to the left.*

at night, as the occasional lights are intended for the assistance of pilots who have local knowledge. Leading lights situated about 1½ cables south-west of the pier are exhibited from half flood to half ebb from 1 March to 30 September when vessels are expected. Front: fixed R. 34 ft. from a round tower. Rear: fixed R. 37 ft. from black column. The two in line at 334° lead clear of rocks off the Ness, but cross the Pole sands. On the beacon on the training bank there is a fixed light W.R.G. sectors 12 ft. Green from 100° to 160°; white to 220°; red to 280°. The Ness is floodlit on the north side during summer months. Occasional fixed green leading lights at 021° are shown at New Quay and lead up the west side of the reach of the river between the Point and Salty Flat. For other lights see chart.

Moorings and Anchorage Avoid anchoring in the entrance as the ebb runs very hard. Anchor (1) outside in settled weather about 2 cables east of the end of the pier in 9 ft. or more seaward; (2) lie, on moorings on application to Harbour Master, or hire moorings if any available from Morgan Giles' yacht yard on west of the Den.

Upper Reaches The river above Shaldon bridge is navigable as far as Newton Abbot at high water by small craft with local knowledge.

101.   *The beacon at high water with the training wall covered. It should be left about 50 yards to port.*

Facilities Water from New Quay. Petrol, oil and chandlery. Morgan Giles yacht yard with patent slipway up to 120 ft. and 9 ft. draft, and several boatyards. Several hotels. Good shops. Early closing Thursday. Launching site for dinghies at Shaldon. At Teignmouth there is access to the river on the north side of the Den, and there is a private launching site at the yacht yard of Morgan Giles Ltd. Ferry from Ferry Point to Shaldon. Yacht clubs: Teign Corinthian Y.C., Shaldon S.C. Buses and main line station for London.

102.   *In the reach between Salty Flat and the Point. Steering N.E. by N. towards the New Quay on left of picture and leaving the yard of Morgan Giles Ltd. to starboard.*

TORQUAY

Plan No. 32

High Water —05 h. 08 m. *Dover.*
Rise 13.6 *ft. springs; 9.8 ft. neaps.*
Depths 21 *ft. to 23 ft. off entrance; 19 ft. between the piers. Inside the outer harbour there is from 8 to 13 ft. alongside the Haldon (east) pier, and from 13 to 15 ft. along the outer area of the Princess (west) pier. In the centre of the harbour the depth is from 7 to 10 ft., but the inner harbour almost dries out at M.L.W.S. except for about 2 ft. along south pier.*

TORQUAY lies in the north-western corner of Torbay. The harbour is convenient and is sheltered, except in onshore winds, which, if strong, can make conditions inside uncomfortable. The town is a large and popular seaside resort and is rather crowded during the holiday season.

Approach and Entrance Approaching from the eastward the church tower on high ground at the back of Babbacombe Bay and the spire of the R.C. church will first be seen. Torbay will next be identified with Hope Nose and the Ore Stone (106 ft.) and Thatcher (134 ft.) rocks on the north side and Berry Head on the south. Entering the north side of the bay note that there

is a sunken outlier about 100 yds. S.W. of Ore Stone, and the Morris Rogue (4 ft. over it) 1½ cables S.E. of the East Shag (35 ft.) rock.

From the southward there are no outlying dangers. The entrance is 80 yds. wide, and craft drawing up to 14 ft. of water can enter or leave at any state of the tide. Inside there is not much room, so enter slowly, or under reduced sail and be prepared to meet excursion vessels, which are frequently leaving the harbour.

Lights South of the entrance a buoy Fl. ev. sec. On the Haldon (east) pier a fixed green light (white over harbour); on Princess (west) pier a fixed red light

103.   *The Ore Stone (outer) and Thatcher rocks are conspicuous on the northern extremity of Torbay. The picture faces north.*

104. *Torquay harbour and entrance showing Princess pier (left), Haldon pier (right) and south pier of the inner drying harbour. Moorings for yachts are shown and also the dinghy slips in outer harbour and the slip in the inner harbour.* [*Photo: Aero Films*]

(white over harbour). On the inner pier there is a fixed white light.

Anchorage and moorings (1) Outside, in offshore winds, good anchorage in line with western breakwater in $1\frac{1}{2}$ to $3\frac{1}{2}$ fathoms. (2) *Inside harbour*. Moor to buoy as directed by the Harbour Master, or temporarily to one of the big harbour moorings. Large yachts lie inside to east and west of entrance, smaller ones farther in. The outer piers are in constant use by pleasure and excursion vessels in summer months, but yachts sometimes lie alongside the wall in inner harbour and dry out.

Facilities Water from tap near dinghy landing on east of outer harbour or in quantity at the Haldon or the south pier. Petrol, oil and chandlery at south pier. Boatbuilders. Scrubbing by arrangement. Launching site at all states of tide on slip on east of outer harbour with car park adjacent (often full); also at slipway in inner harbour, 3 hrs. each side of H.W., by permission of the Harbour Master. Hotels and restaurants of all grades. Excellent shops. Early closing Wednesday or Saturday. Main line station. Buses to all parts and coaches. Ferry to Brixham. Yacht clubs: R. Torbay Y.C., Torquay Corinthian Y.C.

105. *This picture faces north-east towards the south pier of the inner harbour, with dinghy slip and car park to right.*

PAIGNTON

High Water —05 h. 10 m. Dover.
Rise 13½ ft. springs; 10 ft. neaps.
Depths The entrance to the harbour dries out at L.W. Anchorage outside 8 to 15 ft.

PAIGNTON HARBOUR is small in area and the centre is occupied by motor launches and local boats closely moored. The northern quay is used by excursion boats but there is room for yachts to berth and dry out at the quay. It is well provided with facilities.

Approach and Entrance Paignton harbour is on the north side of Roundham Head, which is a prominent red cliff headland in the middle of Torbay. There is a rocky spit running eastward from the East quay. The seaward extremity of the spit is marked by a lattice beacon with a spoil ground topmark. The approach from north-east is simplest. The entrance faces north and is narrow.

Anchorage and Moorings (1) Outside. Anchor in sand or mud well off entrance in 8 to 15 ft. approximately in line with the end of the eastern breakwater and Torquay harbour entrance. This anchorage

106.   *Entrance to Paignton harbour, picture from anchorage to north-east of harbour.*

is sheltered by Roundham Head from the south and south-west and from the west by the general coastline. It is open from north through the east to south. East winds cause an uncomfortable swell and heavy sea at the entrance. There is some swell from passing excursion boats, but the anchorage during prevailing westerly winds is better sheltered than at Brixham or Torquay. (2) Lie along quay inside by arrangement with Harbour Master.

Facilities Water, petrol and oil available at harbour. A few small shops at harbour and all shopping facilities at Paignton, ¼ mile to north-west. Early closing Wednesday. Three boatbuilders at the harbour and yacht chandlers. Launching slips 3 hrs. each side of H.W. and car park. Frequent buses. Main line station at Paignton. Many hotels and restaurants. Yacht Club: Torbay S.C.

107. *Paignton harbour with Torquay and the Thatcher and Ore Stone rocks across the bay.*

BRIXHAM

Plan No. 33

High Water −05 h. 13 m. *Dover.*
Rise 14 *ft. springs;* 10½ *ft. neaps.*
Depths 20 *to* 25 *ft. M.L.W.S. in outer harbour for about* 3 *cables from Breakwater Head; the inner harbour dries out.*

BRIXHAM was famous as a fishing port, and the whole harbour used to be occupied by trawlers and their moorings. The industry had declined but now is prospering again. The big outer harbour is available for yachts which makes it one of the best yachting centres in the West Country. The Brixham Yacht Club is an active one, and hospitable to visiting yachtsmen of recognized clubs. The harbour is sheltered except from the north and Torbay provides a fine sailing area with weak tides and which is open only to the east.

Approach and Entrance Brixham is easy to locate and easy to enter. It lies a mile north-west of Berry Head, which is a headland, sloping at 45°, easy of recognition by day (see photograph) and clearly identifiable at night owing to its lighthouse. The harbour entrance is wide but the end of the breakwater should not be rounded closely when approaching from east as trawlers and excursion launches may be leaving the harbour and be hidden by the breakwater.

Lights Berry Head Light, Gp. Fl. (2) ev. 15 sec. 191 ft. 20 M. At end of breakwater a weak light, occulting red, ev. 15 sec. 3 M. A fixed white light from

108.   *Berry Head and Brixham harbour from north-west, showing breakwater and lighthouse at its end.*

each end of the oil jetty. At the entrance to the inner harbour there is a fixed green light at end of the west pier.

Anchorages (1) Outside in Brixham Roads in about 5 fathoms, or small yachts can find anchorage outside in the corner formed between the inner end of the breakwater and the cliffs extending towards Berry Head, sheltered from west and south. (2) Inside on west side of the harbour east and north-east of the yacht club. The boatman at the yacht club should be consulted. There is not much room between permanent moorings and the fairway except nearer the entrance.

Excursion boats cause violent wash if a yacht is too near fairway. Moorings sometimes available on application to yacht club. (3) Small yachts can anchor in Fishcombe Cove (near the entrance) but this position is dangerous if the wind shifts anywhere north. (4) In the south-east corner of harbour near breakwater. Moorings sometimes available on application to Harbour Master, and Upham's yacht yard have a few sets off the yard, which can be used by permission only. Yachts should be reported to the Harbour Master within 24 hrs. of arrival. In the event of gales from the north, shelter should be sought at Torquay.

109.   *The west side of Brixham harbour, the Brixham Yacht Club (white building with flagstaff on right) and yachts at moorings.*

110. *View from Upham's yacht yard facing north-west. On left the entrance to the inner harbour and west quay, and beyond it the yacht club and yachts at moorings. [Photo: D. Ide]*

Facilities Brixham is particularly well provided with facilities for visiting yachts. Not only are there shops of all kinds (early closing day, Wednesday) but there is Upham's large yacht yard with four slipways and 10-ton hoist. Two other boat repairers. Two scrubbing grids 8 ft. draft and eight scrubbing berths 10 ft. draft by arrangement with Harbour Master. Also crane lift 4 tons at quay head. Compass swinging arrangement with H.M. Sail makers. Water is obtainable at end of west pier, or by permission at the yacht club steps. Petrol at yards or garage. In large quantities water, petrol or oil may be obtained at the bunkering jetty. Yacht chandlers at quay and at Uphams. Launching sites: from south-east corner of outer harbour at all states of tide. Also a small launching way at the west end of the inner harbour alongside the monument, where dinghies can be launched between three-quarter and H.W. Yacht club: Brixham Y.C. Hotels and restaurants. Railway station. Frequent buses to all parts. Frequent excursion boats to Torquay and Paignton.

III.   *Inner harbour, Brixham. [Photo: Aero Films Ltd]*

DARTMOUTH

Plan No. 34

High Water —05 h. 16 m. *Dover.*
Rise 15.4 *ft. springs;* 11.6 *ft. neaps, but much affected by wind conditions.*
Depths *Deep water channel as far as Dittisham, but beyond this there are considerable variations in depth.*

DARTMOUTH is one of the most protected harbours on the south coast. Shelter inside can be found in any weather, and if weatherbound, small yachts will find plenty of water to be explored within the harbour. Dartmouth is a town of character and the upper reaches of the Dart are beautiful. At high water navigation is possible as far as Totnes, some 10 miles up the river, in a vessel of up to 10 ft. draft.

Approach and Entrance Dartmouth lies between the two promontories of Berry Head and the Start (see photographs under Passage Notes), being 5 miles from the former and 7 miles from the latter. The entrance is not conspicuous from seaward, but it can be located by the conspicuous 80 ft. daymark (elevation 500 ft.) above Froward Point, east of the entrance and the craggy Mewstone Rock (115 ft.) and the East Black-stone (125 ft.) off this point (see photographs).

The entrance is deep and well marked but there are dangers on each side. On the east side there are rocks to the west of the Mewstone, and on its south-west the Verticals (dry 6 ft.) and the West Rock with a depth of 3 ft. M.L.W.S. South of Inner Froward Point is the Bear's Tail (dries 2 ft.) and 2¾ cables west of the point is Old Castle Rock (with 6 ft. over it) off which is the black conical Castle Ledge buoy. From about 3 hrs. flood to 3 hrs. ebb the stream sets towards these dangers, which should be given a wide berth. Approaching from the eastward keep the East Blackstone Rock (which is ½ mile east of Mewstone) well open of the Mewstone until Castle Ledge buoy comes in line with Blackstone Point on the west side of entrance.

On the west side of the approach there are rocks a cable off Coombe Point and 3 cables off this point is the Homestone (with 3 ft. over it) marked by R.W. can buoy. To N.N.E. of this Point are the Meg Rocks which dry 3 to 10 ft. Off Blackstone Point there is the Western Blackstone Rock which can be seen as it is 8 ft. high, but there is a sunken off-lier close north-east of it.

The fairway between these dangers is wide so that the approach is easy. In the narrows there are two rocks to avoid on the west side opposite Kingswear Castle, the Checkstone (1 ft. over it) which is marked by a R.W. can buoy and the Kitten rock (6 ft. over it)

112. *Dartmouth Day Beacon situated north of Inner Froward Point. The Mewstone rises behind the yacht. The photograph is taken with the day beacon bearing approximately north, distant 1 mile.*

113. *The Mewstone and associated rocks from the southward.*

S.S.E. of the buoy which lies at the end of a ledge ¾ cable southward of Battery Point. The Kitten rock is on the edge of the fairway, so when approaching the narrows keep nearer to the east side of the channel and steer to give a good berth to the Checkstone buoy. The wind is often baffling and fluky in the narrows and their

114. *Battery Point and Dartmouth Castle on west side of narrows, and the Checkstone buoy.*

115. *Kingswear moorings and anchorage facing south towards the station and ferry.*

approach, but navigation is straightforward after passing the Checkstone and a vessel will proceed up the fairway.

Lights Enter in white sector of Kingswear light on east side of harbour. Fixed W.R.G. 85 ft. 12 M, W. 325° to 331°, R. 325°, to 318°, G. 331° to 343°. The green sector covers dangers to port, and the red those to starboard. Alter course to port when the red sector (289° to 297°) of fixed harbour light is entered and steer for it; thence steer up river between the shore lights of Dartmouth and Kingswear. When leaving Dartmouth steer on stern bearing in red sector of the harbour light or in the F.W. sector of the light a cable north of Kettle rock on east side of river. When the W. sector of Kingswear light is entered steer out in it.

Anchorage and Moorings (1) Outside there is temporary anchorage in settled weather in the range but there is often an uncomfortable swell. It is prohibited in the area between Blackstone Point bearing 291° and Combe Point bearing 343°. (2) Off Warfleet Cove between moorings and fairway. (3) Off Kingswear above the station, though uncomfortable if wind is against the tide. Moorings are available here and for smaller yachts on the Dartmouth side, on application to the Harbour Master. (4) Moorings and berths available at Dart Marina above floating bridge on west side, with petrol, oil, water, yacht yard, hotel and facilities. Marina also has moorings up river off Noss Works. (5) Off or above Old Mill creek on west of river about a mile above Dartmouth clear of R.N. craft but holding ground poor, or on west side opposite Noss Point. (6) Below Dittisham Ferry. (7) Off Galmpton in about 10 ft. of water in the channel east of the mud flat.

Upper Reaches The channel is not marked above Dittisham. It can be navigated to Galmpton with care, but above this the channel is tortuous, the bottom is very uneven and there are mud banks. With the aid of a large scale chart and local knowledge the river can be navigated at H.W. to Totnes.

Facilities Water from water boat and at quays. Petrol and oil. Fuel can also be obtained alongside quay (9 ft. H.W.) by arrangement with Harbour Master. Hotels, good shopping centre—early closing Wednesday. Yacht yards, all facilities and provision boat. Yacht clubs: R. Dart Y.C. (Kingswear), Dartmouth S.C., Dittisham S.C. Boatel with cabins and hire boats. Launching sites: public slipway at Kingswear next R. Dart Y.C., except near L.W.; slipway at Dartmouth dinghy basin, 2 hrs. each side H.W. or at any tide from slipway alongside upper ferry slipway, provided ferry is not obstructed. Station at Kingswear. Buses to all parts.

SALCOMBE

Plan No. 35

High Water —05 *h.* 38 *m. Dover.*
Rise 15.9 *ft. springs;* 12.4 *ft. neaps.*
Depths *On the bar a depth of 5 ft. of water M.L.W.S. may be found by yachtsmen with local knowledge, but strangers should not count on more than 2 ft. M.L.W.S. In the 'Range' (the approach to the bar) there is from 25 to 40 ft. and ¼ mile above the bar there is a deep channel as far as Tosnos Point in the 'Bag'. Above Tosnos Point to Collapit Lake the depths vary from 7 to 14 ft. but strangers may not find the best water. The estuary then shallows, but at three-quarter flood it is possible for vessels drawing 9 ft. to navigate up to Kingsbridge, some 3 miles above Salcombe.*

SOME yachtsmen consider that Salcombe is the best of the West Country ports. It certainly has a claim to this distinction for the harbour is lovely and is well sheltered. It offers many anchorages, and is ideal for day sailing and boating of all kinds, and for family bathing, picnics and walks.

Approach and Entrance The entrance is a simple matter with sufficient rise of tide on the bar and in the absence of strong onshore winds or swell.

The entrance is just to the east of Bolt Head, and some 3 miles west of the Prawle. Bolt Head is a remarkable promontory with a spiked sky line. There are two islets, 'Mewstones', off the Point. A stranger might find some resemblance in profile between the Bolt and the Start, but the latter is a far longer headland and has a white lighthouse on it. See Passage Notes.

Strong southerly winds meeting the ebb at the Bolt set up overfalls which can be avoided by entering from farther east. The only dangers in the approach are rocks in the west side near the Mewstones which should be given a fair berth and on the east side the groups of rocks near the Rickman Rock, which has 10 ft. over it, M.L.W.S., and rocks near the coast farther eastwards.

Whether approaching from west or east it is simplest to alter course northwards about ¼ mile east of the Bolt. As the vessel sails northward, the small Starhole bay will be left to port where the remains of the wreck of the barque *Herzogin Cecilie* lie in the northwest corner under the high cliffs.

A headland on the north of this little bay with a detached rock (the Gt. Eelstone) will be observed. The Cadmus Rocks (2 ft. least water) extend ¾ cable S. ½ E. of Gt. Eelstone and must be avoided. The bar is situated about 3 cables north of the Gt. Eelstone Rock. The exact position is indicated by a large white mark on the land on the port side.

The line of approach from ¼ mile east of the Gt. Mewstone, in transit with the leading beacons, leaves the Gt. Eelstone about 1½ cables to port. The leading marks consist of a red and white beacon with R.W. cage top mark on the Poundstone Rock (dries 12 ft.) and a white beacon with a diamond top mark, situated in front of the left tangent of a big red-roofed house with two gables (see photograph). These bear 000° (N. by E.) and if they cannot be located, a compass bearing on the left tangent of the house should suffice.

The bar is dangerous in strong onshore winds especially with wind against an ebb tide, and has depths ranging from about 2 to 5 ft. M.L.W.S. The bar should not be attempted under the conditions mentioned nor should it be crossed when a swell is running in until there is ample rise of tide over it. It is here that a life-

116. *The leading beacons should be kept almost in line with the left tangent of the red-roofed house with two gables.*

boat was lost. The entrance and bar is protected by land from the west and in normal conditions presents no difficulties.

Once over the bar the vessel will leave to port the Bass Rock (dries 3 ft.) off the next point, and to starboard the Wolf Rock (dries 2 ft.) marked by a black conical buoy. Course will then be altered to leave to port the Poundstone and two beacons off Sandhill Point and to starboard the beacon marking the Blackstone Rocks. There is an unmarked reef fringing the next headland (Biddlehead) and the Ram Rock on the east side, but otherwise the reach to Salcombe is plain sailing near mid-channel.

Lights There are no leading lights, but there is a fixed red light on Salcombe jetty.

Anchorage and Moorings In the range outside the bar during offshore winds in settled weather, in 5 fathoms about 3 cables east of the Great Eelstone Rock. (2) Outside in Starhole Bay but avoid wreck extending a cable off north-west corner, in 3 to 5 fathoms. (3) Large yachts usually bring up off the Marine Hotel, but there is a sea here in south-west winds. (4) Off the mud flats between Salcombe and Snapes Point. (5) Off Ditch End, on south side of the channel east of Salcombe, nearly opposite the entrance of the Bag. Convenient landing here, then short walk to ferry boat but moorings now occupy best positions. Take soundings to find position between deep channel and steep edge of Southpool Lake. (6) In the Bag, about ¾ mile north-west of Salcombe. Moorings can usually be hired here, but if anchoring take care to keep clear of moorings, with which the anchorage is crowded. (7) In pool beyond shallow entrance of Frogmore Creek in 6 to 8 ft.

In selecting an anchorage, wind and weather must be considered. The anchorages off Salcombe can be uncomfortable in bad weather when the Bag is usually preferred, although it is sometimes crowded and is a long way from the facilities of Salcombe.

Creeks The arms and creeks provide a pretty and interesting cruising area for dinghies and shallow draft boats at H.W., but a large scale chart is needed.

Southpool Lake, which joins the main channel opposite Salcombe has uneven depths and the pools are occupied by moorings.

Frogmore Creek, which joins on the east side above Tosnos Point, also has an uneven bottom with depths ranging from 1 to 8 ft.

The upper reaches of the main channel are marked by posts on the mud on the port hand above Gerston Point and are navigable at high water to Kingsbridge. Balcombe Lake, the fork bearing towards the northeast at High House Point is shallow and is crossed by a road bridge.

Facilities Water and garage for petrol and oil near landing slip. Pontoon and car park, or water from ferryman, yards or water boat. Hotels and many shops. Early closing Thursday. Six yacht or boat yards. Chandlers. Grid. New public pontoon for landing at Salcombe. Launching slip 2 hrs. each side of H.W. and car park, though often crowded. Yacht club: Salcombe Y.C. The Island Cruising Club invites visiting yachtsmen to use its clubhouse at N.E. end of Salcombe. Moorings can often be provided for large and medium yachts, particularly mid-week. Club maintains scheduled launch service between Salcombe and the Bag. A "Z" signal will summon the launch. Buses hourly to Kingsbridge where there is a station.

HOPE COVE

THIS cove lies just to the northward of Bolt Tail, and affords fair anchorage for yachts and ships of all sizes during winds from N.N.E. to S.E. in depths ranging from 5 to 2 fathoms. There are some ledges in the inner cove, and there is a drying harbour formed by a breakwater for boats. Three hotels. Village. Early closing Thursday.

117.   *Salcombe as seen from the entrance of Southpool Lake.*

RIVER AVON

Plan No. 36

High Water —05 h. 36 m. Dover.
Rise at Entrance 16.1 ft. springs; 12.5 ft. neaps. *Inside river about 6 ft. less rise.*

Depths 3 ft. to 6 ft. in anchorage east of Borough Island. Bar practically dries. Depths in river 1 to 3 ft., except in pools.

THE ENTRANCE of the River Avon is easy to locate as it is ½ mile east of the conspicuous Borough Island, 2 miles west of Bolt Tail. The entrance should be approached only in fine settled weather and offshore winds. The anchorage at Borough Island may be used by keel yachts under suitable conditions. Although there is plenty of water in the river at H.W. the river is difficult to navigate without local knowledge, as the sands shift, the channel is not marked, the banks rise steeply in places and the streams attain 6 knots. It could be attempted on the last of the flood in a shallow draft yacht after a previous survey by dinghy. The following notes and the plan serve as a rough guide only.

118. *The anchorage east of Borough Island. The yacht touched bottom at L.W. but there is more water close to the inner of the large rocks, just to the left of the figures in the foreground.*

To the south-east of Borough Island there is a line of rocks which extends over $2\frac{1}{2}$ cables, gradually lowering in height from above-water rocks near the island to a rock with 4 ft. over it at M.L.W.S. at the extreme end. The approach should accordingly be made in the eastern part of the bay between Borough Island and Longstone Point, heading towards the group of houses shown on the right of Photograph No. 119, which leads towards the river entrance. When an imaginary line extended from the reef south-east of Borough Island has been crossed, course may be altered for the north side of the hotel on Borough Island, leaving the line of rocks to port, to reach the anchorage. The sands dry out between the island and Bigbury-on-Sea and to the north of the anchorage. This consists of little more than a pool, 6 ft. to 3 ft. with the rocks close southward and sands drying rapidly to the northward. The position is shown in Photograph No. 118, but the yacht grounded at L.W. and should be closer to the innermost large rock above the people on the sands. The anchorage is sheltered in northerly winds, the island protects it from the west and the rocks

119. *The entrance to the river is roughly in line with the two right hand houses on the hill.*

give some shelter from south, but it would be a dangerous place to be caught out in if the wind backed fresh to south or south-east. Shops at Bigbury-on-Sea. Early closing Tuesday.

The position of the entrance of the river varies, but in 1960 was roughly in line with the two white houses on the right—Photograph No. 119—but the direction is stated to have changed more towards the eastward. It has shelving sands each side of the entrance, but there are occasional rocks on the sands on the port hand. As the cliffs are approached the channel be-comes closely confined by steep banks, and the bend to the east and south-east is shown in Photograph No. 120. There are white marks on the cliffs at bends, to E. and S.E., but neither marks nor bends are clear. The stream attains 6 knots. There is anchorage in 3 ft. and a sandy beach for boats able to take the ground, at Lower Cellars, and an 8 ft. pool at Bantham but little room to anchor (provisions, water, inn and P.O.). The river is navigable at H.W. as far as Aveton Gifford where there is a 5 ft. pool (water, petrol, oil and provisions).

120. *The turn to the eastward in the river channel.*

RIVER ERME

Plan No. 37

High Water —05 *h.* 27 *m. Dover.*
Rise at Entrance 16.1 *ft. springs;* 12.5 *ft. neaps.*
Depths *From* 3¼ *to* 1½ *fathoms on west side of inlet. Bar dries out. In the river there is a pool above the breakwater with* 3 *to* 6 *ft. M.L.W.S. At H.W. springs there is about* 11 *ft. and at H.W. neaps about* 7 *ft. in the channel.*

THE RIVER ERME is situated in Bigbury Bay, about a mile west of Erme Head. It should only be approached during settled offshore winds and in the absence of swell. There is a temporary anchorage outside in 18 to 9 ft., but keel yachts should only enter the river with local knowledge, and even light draft boats should enter with caution as the sands on the bar are liable to shift. It is best to obtain pilotage from a local boat or survey the bar at L.W. from the dinghy before attempting entrance.

In the approach from eastward Wells Rock (4 ft. over it) ½ mile southwards of Erme Head must be

121.   *Entrance of River Erme. Owen Hill on left and Muckstone Point on right.*

avoided. The entrance to the bay or inlet lies between Battisborough Island on the west and Erme Head on the east. The centre is obstructed by the two groups of St. Mary's Rocks which dry at L.W. and farther seaward lies the Edward Rock with 6 ft. over it M.L.W.S. With local knowledge and sufficient rise of tide entry is made between the groups of rocks, but strangers will find it easier to follow up the western shore close to the cluster of high rocks known as Battisborough Island. The water is deep up to the cove west of Owen Hill (see photograph) where temporary anchorage may be found in 9 ft., but the depths rapidly decrease beyond this towards the bar. The position of the bar alters from time to time and the river channel runs between sands, but ½ mile beyond Owen Hill there is a breakwater on the west side where there is the best water. Beyond it lies Salmon's Pool, which although narrow has depths of 3 ft. to 6 ft. and affords anchorage for light draft yachts. No facilities.

122. *The anchorage south of Owen Hill. Further northward the depths rapidly decrease.*

Plan No. 38a and 38b

High Water —05 h. 37 m. Dover.
Rise 16.1 ft. springs; 12.5 ft. neaps.
Depths 7 ft. M.L.W.S. best water in the channel *south of the bar off Season Point, 4 to 5 ft. north-west of the outer beacon, 7 to 13 ft. inside as far as Yealm Hotel. In the north channel to within 3 cables of Steer Point the depths are from 5 to 10 ft. and the easterly channel (Newton Ferrers Creek) dries out.*

123.   *The Mewstone from south-west, showing general features of Wembury Bay and the entrance to the Yealm. Wembury Church tower is seen over the right hand corner of the Mewstone.*

124.   *Wembury Church and tower.*

THE YEALM is one of the most beautiful harbours on the south coast. The anchorage is sheltered and the entrance easy, except in strong onshore winds. It is not quite so well provided with facilities as Salcombe, but no cruise on the south coast would be complete without putting into this secluded river.

Approach and Entrance The entrance is rough in strong onshore winds from the south-west, but under normal conditions with adequate rise of tide it is easy enough. Wembury Bay, which forms the entrance, lies between Wembury Point on the north and Yealm Head on the south-east. From Wembury Head there are rocks and ledges extending ½ mile south towards the conspicuous Mewstone Island, 194 ft. high. On the south-west side of the Mewstone lies the Little Mewstone rock (48 ft.) which has an offlying rock 50 yds. off it awash at L.W. Altogether the rocks or shoals extend 2 cables south-west of the Mewstone, and were formerly marked by a conical buoy. In this vicinity there are tide rips when the wind is across the stream. A quarter of a mile eastward of the Mewstone lie the Inner (dry 10 ft.) and Outer (dry 4 ft.) Slimers.

Approaching from the northward or westward the

125. *Approaching the entrance, half way between the line of the transit marks on the right and the shore. The second pair of marks can be seen on left of picture to right of the clump of trees.*

126.   *Near approach to first pair of leading marks.*

Mewstone should be given a berth of at least ¼ mile before standing in towards Gara Point, to ensure that the Slimers are left to the northward (port hand). Dangers on the starboard hand are the ledges off Gara Point and the Western and Eastern Ebb rocks about 3 cables west and south-west of the Point, and the ledges extending a cable westward of Mouthstone Point on the south side of the river entrance. When Wembury Church (on the north side of the bay) bears north-east steer for it until the following marks are opened up.

As the entrance is opened up, a cottage will be seen on Misery Point (the inner point on the south side of the river) and below it, above Cellar Bay, a pair of leading beacons at 089° with black and white boards. Bring these into line. After leaving Mouthstone ledges to starboard keep slightly south of the transit, steering

midway between their transit and the shore on the starboard hand.

Approaching from the eastward give Gara Head a berth of about ½ mile. Wembury Church (situated about a mile east of Wembury Point) is the leading mark and when it is bearing 002° (N. by E.) the Ebb rocks will be left to starboard, but N.N.E. gives better clearance. Hold on until the leading marks above-mentioned have been seen. Then alter course to their transit and proceed as before.

The bar lies southward from Season Point and now extends as far as the transit of the beacons, leaving 7 ft. M.L.W.S. between the transit and the shore. When close to the leading marks in Cellar Bay course has again to be altered, and the next leading beacons (square red and white) will be seen to the north-east on the north shore. These lead through the first bend in the channel at 045° but cross an inner arm of the bar with only 4 to 5 ft. M.L.W.S. After that the river is clearly defined and it is merely necessary to keep near mid-channel taking care only to leave to port the R.W. buoy on the spit off Warren Point (the next point on the north side).

Above Warren Point, the Newton Ferrers creek opens out on the east side. It is wide but dries out at L.W. The River Yealm itself continues above Warren Point first in a N.N.W. direction and then bears through north to north-east. The bottom is uneven, with depths of 12 ft. to 8 ft. for a mile, but with shallower patches.

Sailing school boats practise near the entrance, and include beginners, who should be given consideration.

Anchorage and Moorings The Yealm has become so popular that moorings are laid in all the best parts. It is possible to hire moorings on application to the Harbour Master but generally room to anchor can be found. Holding ground in the river is poor and yachts should lay to two anchors, which should be buoyed if close to moorings. (1) Anchor outside, south-west of Misery Point in Cellar Bay in 6 ft. sheltered from east and south and in settled weather only. (2) Anchor in the pool west of Warren Point, where an area has been cleared of moorings. Moorings are occasionally available on application to the Harbour Master. (3) Note

127. *The second pair of leading marks are on the north side to the right of the clump of trees. The rock on the right of the picture indicates the foot of Misery Point.*

that anchorage is prohibited between the lower limit of oyster beds north of Madge Point and the upper limit east of Steer Point.

Facilities Water at private tap by Ferry Cottage near slip, or free at tap on ferry steps under Yealm Hotel. Stores and post office at Newton Ferrers and Noss Mayo, also petrol and oil. Early closing day, Thursday. Scrubbing can be arranged; two boat-builders. Hotels. Yealm Yacht Club and Newton Ferrers Sailing School. Launching sites: (1) Free slip for launching at Bridgend 2½ hrs. either side of H.W. (2) At the Brook, Newton Ferrers, same hours. (3) Also at Riverside road west 3½ hrs. either side of H.W.S. or 4½ hrs. at H.W.N. Harbour Master at Newton Ferrers. Buses to Plymouth. Also steamers in summer during good weather. Station, Plymouth.

128. *Ferry Point. Newton Ferrers. Photo from spit buoy off Warren Point. The Yealm hotel left of centre. The most likely place to find room to anchor is between the camera viewpoint and the hotel.*

PLYMOUTH

Plan Nos. 39, 40, 41, 42

High Water −05 h. 49 m. Dover.
Rise 16.0 ft. springs; 12.4 ft. neaps, but much influenced by wind and rain conditions.
Depths A deep water harbour used by large ships.

PLYMOUTH is a naval and commercial port. The well-known anchorages are rather too exposed for small yachts in bad weather, but shelter can be found in the docks or up the rivers, with frequent bus services connecting with centre of the town. Cawsand at the west entrance and the Yealm River to the east are two of the pleasant anchorages conveniently near the town of Plymouth. Inside the harbour is the River Tamar running northwards above Saltash, which is navigable and sheltered. The Tavy joins the Tamar about $1\frac{1}{4}$ miles above Saltash. This is a pretty river and though yachts cannot pass under the bridge it is navigable by small craft at H.W.

Below Saltash the St. Germans (or Lynher) River joins the Hamoaze and extends in a westerly direction. The river is deep for about 2 miles and is navigable. Large scale charts are required for navigation in these rivers. The harbour has developed considerably of recent years as a yacht and dinghy centre and there are more yacht and sailing clubs than in any other south-west centre. It is under the jurisdiction of the Queen's Harbour Master. There are bye-laws and prohibited anchorages situated principally in the main fairways.

Approach and Entrance Plymouth Sound lies between Penlee Point on the west and Wembury Point (off which lies the Mewstone) on the east. Within the Sound is a long low breakwater in the centre with channels each side of it. The principal approach to the harbour is through the western channel but the eastern channel is also navigable by day.

The Eddystone rocks and lighthouse are situated 10 miles S.W. by S. of the eastern entrance, and the approach to Plymouth is conspicuous. From the westward a vessel will first pass Rame Head which appears as an almost conical promontory with the ruins of a chapel at its summit. A mile and a quarter east is Penlee Point, a low headland with a turreted beacon tower. The Draystone rocks (over most of which there is 8 ft.) extend $\frac{1}{4}$ mile to the south-east of Penlee Point, and are marked by a R.W. can buoy which should be left to port. The western entrance lies only $1\frac{1}{2}$ miles ahead, between Mount Edgecumbe and the breakwater. If the wind is light and off the land there are often pockets of calm or variable winds. After passing through the western entrance, Drake's Island will lie

129. *Plymouth breakwater at high water and West Head lighthouse. Staddon Heights in background.*

130. *Drake's Island from south and to right Plymouth Hoe.*

to the northward, distant 1¼ miles. The main fairway leads north-east and is marked on the port hand by the R.W. New Grounds and Melampus buoys and thence through the Asia Pass towards the famous Plymouth Hoe (front). Yachts need not keep to the big ship fairway and can leave the buoys on the wrong side by reference to the chart. For principal buoys within the harbour see chart.

There is a short cut to the Hamoaze across the rocky ledge between Drake's Island and the Mount Edgecumbe shore known as 'The Bridge'. This channel has 6 ft. M.L.W.S. and is buoyed, but is not very clear to strangers.

From the eastward the Mewstone (194 ft.) and the rocks south-west of it will be left to starboard. Next the Shagstone, off Renney Point (a nearly square rock 4 ft. high marked by a black beacon surmounted by a globe) should be given a good berth as the tide may be setting across the rocks between it and the shore. The vessel continues northward passing between the breakwater (beacon at east extremity) and Staddon Point, leaving the coastline to starboard until the channel between Drake's Island and Mount Batten is approached. Here course may be altered to take the Asia Pass north-east of Drake's Island or the Smeaton Pass eastward of it or, if bound for the Barbican or Cattewater, hold on to Mount Batten breakwater end leaving it to starboard and the Mallard Shoal (13 ft.) to port.

The passes are used by large ships, and as will be seen on the chart yachts need not adhere to them.

LIGHTS

Plymouth Breakwater. West Head: Lt. Fl. W.R. ev. 10 sec. 13 M. Elevation 63 ft. White from 262° through west to 208°; red elsewhere. Also lower Iso. W. light 4 sec. from 031° to 039°, 39 ft. Fog signal: bell ev. 15 sec.

Penlee Point. Fog signal: reed ev. 10 sec. *Buoys: Port Hand Buoys:* Draystone Gp. Fl. (2) 5 sec. Queen's Ground Gp. Fl. (2) R. New Ground Fl. R. Melampus Fl. (R.). At night enter by the western channel, and keep lookout for unlit buoys.

Anchorage and Moorings As Plymouth is a large harbour, the selection of an anchorage depends on wind direction and weather conditions. It is always wise to buoy the anchor. (1) Outside. Cawsand Bay is an excellent anchorage in winds from south-west to north-west. It has gradually shelving shores and offers good holding ground. (2) Off the north side of Drake's Island. Good holding, but exposed in unsettled weather. (3) Moorings off the Royal Western Yacht Club, or anchorage near in calm weather. (4) In the Cattewater (the easterly channel to the north of Mount Batten). Either off the Barbican on eastern side leading to Sutton Pool, in the Pool where moorings can sometimes be hired. Moorings are also available on application to the

131.   *Royal Western Yacht Club of England (with flagstaff) and Plymouth Hoe.*

132.   *Entrance to Mill Bay dock is east of the conspicuous building.*

yacht yard in Clovelly Bay, west of Turnchapel Point. If anchoring in the Cattewater (prohibited ½ mile S. of bridge) buoy the anchor. (5) Anchor in Barn Pool, which is a bay sheltered from the west by Mount Edgecumbe. The bay is very deep, so work in well towards the shore and let go in about 2½ fathoms. Here also buoy the anchor as there is wreckage on bottom. Reverse eddy close inshore. (6) Off Cremyll, near the ferry, but the stream is strong. (7) Off Torpoint in the Hamoaze above the ferry-landing and sewer outfall, marked by a noticeboard, in 2 fathoms. Avoid fouling moorings. (8) Mill Bay dock. Subject to permission of the Dock Master (east side of entrance) and payment of dock dues, yachts may lock through near H.W. into the inner basin and lie alongside the quay. Entry signals: three black balls or three green lights vertical. Waiting trots in outer basin. There is complete shelter in the basin, all facilities and dock police in charge. Mill Bay dock is the best position for preparing to 'go foreign'. Provisions and bonded stores near by and customs. Local shops and not far from centre of town. If leaving the yacht, arrangements for caretaking may be made.

Tamar River Above Tor Point the river continues wide and deep and there are naval and reserve ships at moorings. Two miles up the river St. Germans River joins it on the west side, and ¾ mile beyond it is spanned by the high railway bridge and the new road suspension bridge at Saltash. The entrance of the River Tavy lies 1¼ miles above the bridge, and here the river shallows to 8 ft. near the starboard hand buoy, and there are wide expanses of shallows on the west side. It gradually deepens again though the bottom is uneven (from 1½ to 3 fathoms) and the river is spanned by high tension cables (100 ft. and 63 ft.). Above this point soundings are unreliable, but after crossing a 5 ft. shoal the river deepens to 2 or 3 fathoms off Cargreen. Above Cargreen the channel requires local knowledge as the best water is narrow between mud shoals and is unmarked. The upper reaches are navigable by shallow draft boats near H.W. Principal anchorages: (1) Saltash on west side below the car ferry or above the bridge in 2 fathoms or more. Anchorage prohibited in vicinity of water mains and cables. Facilities at Saltash. (2) Off Cargreen. Water. facilities and inn.

St. Germans or Lynher River The river is entered from the Tamar on the north side leaving to port the flats and Beggars Island. It is buoyed as far as Forder Lake off which there is 8 ft. Beyond this the bottom is uneven, with shallow reaches and deep pools such as the Dandy Hole south of Earth Hill. Above Earth Hill the river is navigable in the dinghy or in shallow draft boats near H.W. Principal anchorages: (1) Off the bay east of Jupiter Point. (2) Off Forder Lake west of ferry in 8 ft. to 10 ft. (3) In Dandy Hole in 7 ft. to 19 ft. on south side of river south of Earth Hill and north of

Warren Wood. This anchorage can only be reached at half flood, and soundings should be taken to find the edges of the pool. Two anchors necessary to restrict swinging and no facilities.

River Tavy This shallow river is not available for yachts as it is spanned near the entrance by high tension lines (40 ft. clearance) and by a railway bridge. There are extensive mud flats, but the river is pretty and navigable by dinghy or on the flood by shallow draft boats.

Facilities at Plymouth Plymouth provides all facilities for anything from a dinghy to a man-of-war. There are several yacht yards of which Mashford's at Cremyll is best known. Yacht clubs: R. Western Y.C. of England, R. Plymouth Corinthian Y.C., West Hoe S.C., Mayflower S.C., Laira S.C., Tamar River S.C., Saltash S.C., Torpoint Mosquito S.C., Cawsand Bay S.C. Launching site: the City Council has built a dinghy park alongside the Mayflower S.C., Barbican, which will accommodate about 300 dinghies. The Royal Western Y.C. and R.P.C.Y.C. have also a private slip for club members. Station and express railway services. Good shopping facilities. Early closing day, Wednesday.

Plan No. 43

High Water −05 *h.* 45 *m. Dover.*
Rise 17 *ft. springs;* 13.6 *ft. neaps.*
Depths *Harbour and entrance dries out, but in the harbour there is* 10 *to* 15 *ft. M.H.W.S. and* 7 *to* 12 *ft. at M.H.W.N. In anchorage* 6 *ft. to* 15 *ft. M.L.W.S.*

LOOE lies some 9 miles west of Rame Head and about 8 miles east of Fowey. The harbour which dries at L.W. is not recommended in bad weather, and the entrance is dangerous in south-easterly gales. It is unsuitable for any yacht that cannot take the ground, or lie against a quay, but the anchorage is a good one during offshore winds and is partially protected from the south-west by Looe Island. Though crowded with visitors in summer months, the town is a pleasant one, and the hiring of boats and motor trips form a local summer industry.

Approach and Entrance Looe is easy to locate because Looe Island (St. George's Island) is conspicuous off the entrance. The principal danger in the approach from the westward are the Rennies Rocks which extend south-east and eastward of Looe Island.

To clear them keep the beacon on Gribbin Head open of the cliffs at Nealand Point (west of Polperro) until the tower of the church at East Looe is well open east of the pier end. There are tidal rips south of Looe Island and the Rennies which in bad weather may be avoided by keeping farther seaward. For strangers there is no passage between Looe Island and the mainland. Approaching from the eastward, leave the red can buoy marking Knight Errant Patch (21 ft.) and the Sherberetry Rocks (19 ft.) to the northward though these shoals may be crossed in fine weather by yachts. Course may then be steered from the buoy to the harbour entrance at 304°. If beating in give a good offing to the Rennies Rocks and on near approach to the harbour entrance avoid the Needles Eye, Chimney Rock and other rocks south of the entrance, and the Pen Rock to the north. See chart for soundings. The harbour entrance dries 1 ft. M.L.W.S. Enter with sufficient rise of tide. Off east quay there is a reverse eddy on the flood. There is a coastguard station on east side, from which storm signals are exhibited. Near by a red flag is flown from a flagstaff when conditions in the bay are dangerous to shore boats.

Lights Lt. Occ. W.R. 3 sec. 10 M. at end of pier. Fog siren (2) 30 sec. sounded during fog when fishing and other vessels are at sea. Sectors: white 013° to 207°; red to 267°; white to 313°; red to 332°; obscured elsewhere. Enter at night in white sector 268° to 313°; but note this sector includes the Sherbeterry Rocks and Knight Errant Patch (least depth 19 ft.) and the unlit buoy.

Anchorage and Harbour Anchorage in the

133.   *Looe (St. George's) Island and Rennies rocks from east-south-east.*

134.   *Looe showing entrance, river and west quay. Yachts should anchor seaward of the launches in foreground.*
       [*Photo: Aero Pictorial*]

roadstead is good except in onshore winds or swell, or at high water when the wind is blowing through the gap between Looe Island and the mainland. There is wash from passenger launches and motor boats, as the roadstead is much used by pleasure boats. There are moorings for local craft off the rocks on the south side. The usual transit for anchorage is with the pierhead in line with St. Nicholas Church on west side of harbour though this is difficult to locate. As the ebb runs fiercely out of the harbour and this torrent is felt for some distance seaward, anchorage to northward of the line of the harbour entrance may be found better with the pierhead bearing about west by north, but keep well clear of the Pen Rock which lies a cable north-east of the pier. Depths range from 12 ft. seaward down to 5 ft. a cable off the pierhead. From the anchorage it is a long row in the dinghy to the harbour, except at neaps when it is possible to bring up closer in.

135. *Photograph taken from the bridge facing south at H.W., showing fishing vessels at east quay.*

Within the harbour there are long quays with 10 to 13 ft. M.H.W.S. on the eastern side and 6 to 11 ft. M.H.W.S. on the western. The harbour is often crowded by fishing vessels, and pleasure craft and boats, but the Harbour Master will direct to a berth.

Facilities Water at quays or fish market. Petrol and oil. Hotels and restaurants. Many shops. Early closing Thursday. Boatbuilders and repairers and scrubbing. Launching site and car park on east side near flagstaff. Station and bus services. Yacht Club: Looe S.C.

Plan No. 44

High Water —05 *h.* 39 *m. Dover.*
Rise 17 *ft. springs;* 13.6 *ft. neaps.*
Depths *Harbour dries out but has* 11 *ft. at M.H.W.S. and* 5 *ft. at M.H.W.N. Deepens to* 20 *ft. outside.*

POLPERRO is a small drying harbour 3 miles west of Looe and 5 miles east of Fowey. It lies at the end of an inlet between the cliffs extending about 3 cables in a north-westerly direction, and is protected by an outer pier and two inner piers between which is the entrance. This is only 32 ft. wide and in bad weather can be closed by baulks of timber. Polperro is a fishing village principally engaged in mackerel, pilchard and line fishing. There is no chart of the harbour. The plan is

136.   *Entrance to Polperro opening up.*

137.   *Polperro. [Photo: Aero Films]*

based on a survey by Captains Williams and Bell, R.N. in 1857, coupled with observations of the Harbour Master in 1961. There appears to be little alteration during the last 100 years.

Approach and Entrance Approach should be made from a south-easterly direction when the harbour piers open up. As is shown on the chart, there are rocks extending off the headland on the west side of the entrance and there are also rocks at the foot of the cliffs on the east side. There is deep water up to the entrance of the inlet except for a patch named The Polca which lies a cable S.E. of the entrance and has a depth of only 4 ft. over it. At the entrance there is a patch in mid-channel with a depth of 9 ft. over it, after which the depth increases before shallowing gradually towards the harbour entrance. The approach is dangerous in south-east or southerly winds or when a swell is running in. Once the entrance is gained the inlet is protected from south-west through west to north-east.

Keep in mid-channel when within the inlet and approach the entrance (with sufficient rise of tide) leaving the outer pier well to starboard and steering mid-way between the inner piers.

Lights and Signals Spy-house Point east of the harbour entrance. Fixed white. Vis. 8 M. Elevation 100 ft. On west pierhead fixed white. Vis. 4 M. Elevation 14 ft. When the harbour entrance is closed, a red light is substituted for white at the pierhead and by day a black ball is hoisted.

Anchorage and Harbour Mooring buoys are laid just outside the harbour for mooring while waiting for the tide. There is also room to anchor. There are moorings inside the harbour but these are of use only to yachts equipped with legs, as the harbour dries out a foot or two at L.W. springs. Berths alongside quay subject to requirements of fishing vessels. Fees 4s. per entry.

Facilities Water at fish market and on the quays. Petrol and oil obtainable. Several small hotels. Shops. Early closing Saturday, but usually open during summer months. Frequent buses to Looe and occasional to Polruan and Fowey. Harbour Master. Launching site on sloping beach at head of harbour.

FOWEY

High Water —05 h. 56 m. *Dover.*
Rise 16.7 *ft. springs;* 13.3 *ft. neaps.*
Depths 17 *to* 22 *ft. in the entrance up to Polruan. In the river there is a least depth in the deep channel of* 20 *ft. so far as Wiseman Stone, but above this it soon shallows.*

FOWEY is an attractive west country port. It has a good harbour, available at all states of the tide and sheltered from all but southerly gales. At such times there is a swell in the harbour, but shelter will be found farther up the river. The upper reaches offer pleasant dinghy excursions, though a look out should be kept for squalls from steep slopes and sudden openings.

Approach and Entrance Approaching from the eastward there is the dangerous Udder Rock (dries 2 ft.) situated 3 miles east of the entrance. This is marked by a red bell buoy, and there are no dangers between this rock and the entrance other than rocks

138.   *Fowey. East side of entrance and Punch Cross on right.*

fringing the shore. Fowey would not be very easy to identify from seaward but for the daymark on Gribbin see page 213 → Head, 1¼ miles south-west of the entrance, which must not be confused with the old tower on Pencarro Head, 2 miles east of Fowey. The Gribbin Beacon (see Passage Notes) is a red and white tower 84 ft. high standing at an elevation of 250 ft. on a lofty headland, and is a conspicuous landmark when approaching from any direction.

From the westward avoid the Cannis Rock (dries 14 ft.), some 4 cables south-eastward from Gribbin Head. There are dangers south of the head so far as the Cannis Rock. There is a red can buoy off this rock, but to clear the danger keep the cross on Dodman Point open southward of Gwineas Rock, the 26 ft. high rock north-east of Dodman Point. Bearing of Dodman, 225° true.

Once past the Cannis alter course for the entrance, but as there are rocky ledges off the shore west of the entrance give this side a good berth until close to the entrance. Here the only dangers are the Punch Cross ledge on the east side, marked by a cross 120 ft. from its western extremity (which should therefore be given a wide berth) and the Lamp Rock nearly a cable within on the same side. Fowey is considered a good port to run for, but the entrance is of course very rough during onshore gales, and the seas break heavily in the approach with an ebb tide running against strong

139. *Fowey. Polruan Point and Punch Cross at L.W.: they should be given a wide berth.*

140. *Fowey river with Fowey on left and Polruan on right.*
[Photo: Aero Films]

southerly winds.

Lights Fowey lighthouse, S.W. of St. Catherine's Point: Lt. Fl. ev. 5 sec. 11 M. Red sectors cover the dangers east and west. Approach in the white sector until the orange sector of Whitehouse Point, within the entrance, is picked up; Occ. Or. 12½ sec. 6 M. Enter the harbour in this sector 017° to 037°, but note that in the approach the unlit Cannis buoy lies within the west side of sector and that St. Catherine's Point should be given a good berth. Once within the harbour the shore lights will be seen and there is a light F.R. on Whitehouse jetty, which should be given a good berth to avoid the unlit landing slip.

Anchorage and Moorings The river and harbour is under the control of the Harbour Master, who endeavours to meet the requirements of owners, though in the high season the most convenient berths are not always available. The harbour is used by large steamers, and yachts must not anchor in the fairway or in the main swinging ground which lies between the entrance to Pont Pill on the eastern side and the Whitehouse to Fowey town quay on the western side. Anchorages: (1) Five visitor's moorings off R. Fowey Y.C., which welcomes visiting yachtsmen. (2) Anywhere in the area off Polruan clear of moorings in 1½ to 2 fathoms east of a line approximately from 100 yds. east of Polruan

141. *Polruan.*

Point to the white can buoy south-west of Penleath Point. This anchorage is rough on the ebb tide in strong south and south-west winds. (3) In the pool above Wiseman Point in 12 to 15 ft. This is a secure anchorage, though during gales there are fierce squalls blowing down from the hills. Anchor clear of moorings which occupy the best positions and note the buoys marking the limit of the oyster beds, wherein anchorage must be avoided, except in emergency. When proceeding up the river to Wiseman Pool look out for Carn Rock in the bend above Fowey, red can buoy to be left to port.

Upper Reaches No difficulties are presented in sailing up the river as far as $\frac{1}{2}$ mile above Wiseman Point, but yachts under sail will find the wind heads and is fluky in some reaches. Near Bodmin Pill the channel becomes narrow and shallow and most of the river dries out at L.W. It is navigable by shallow draft boats at high water as far as Lostwithiel, as also Penpoll and Larryn creeks on the east side. These reaches are pretty and reward an excursion in the dinghy.

Facilities Landing at Town quay. Water from R. Fowey Y.C. steps or the Town quay pump. It can also

142.   *Fowey. The anchorage above Wiseman Stone.*

be obtained in quantity from mains at British Railways China Clay quay by prior arrangement with the Fowey Borough Engineer. Petrol and oil obtainable. Hotels and good shops. Early closing Wednesday or Saturday. Customs, Harbour Master and Lloyd's agent. Three yacht or boat yards. Scrubbing by arrangement at Mixtow Pill hard. Yacht clubs: Royal Fowey Y.C., Fowey S.C., Fowey Gallants Club. Buses to St. Austell. Launching site at Bodinnick ferry slipway, but not between 8 a.m. and dusk when ferry is operating. Also from Caffa Mill car park (near old station) and at Polruan. Water, hotel, small shops. Early closing Wednesday. Launching site: slipway at quay with car park adjacent.

POLKERRIS, PAR, CHARLESTOWN, PENRUAN

BETWEEN Mevagissey and Fowey there are four harbours which are unsuitable for deep-keeled yachts but of which mention should be made to make this book complete. The following notes have been taken by kind permission from *The Pilot's Guide to the English Channel*, published by Imray, Laurie, Norie and Wilson Ltd. In offshore winds and settled weather a yacht can anchor well to seaward of the harbours and they can be visited by dinghy.

Polkerris Situated 1½ miles north-west of Gribbin Head, in north-east corner of Tywardreath Bay. Bottom dries 30 yds. beyond pier and harbour is practically disused.

Par Situated 2 miles north-west of Gribbin Head, formed by two piers. Entrance 125 ft. wide, 14 ft. M.H.W.S., 10 ft. M.H.W.N. as far as the inner pier. Dries out at L.W. for about 3 cables nearly as far as Callyvardor Rocks to the south-east. These rocks cover at one-third flood, but are marked on west by an iron beacon. Harbour is used for the china clay trade and is entirely commercial.

Charlestown Situated 2 miles north of Black Head in north-west corner of St. Austell Bay. Formed between two piers, and has a tidal basin at top. Depths 14 ft. M.H.W.S. and 10 ft. M.H.W.N. Dries 200 ft. beyond entrance and dangerous to approach during onshore winds or swell.

Penruan Situated about 1 mile north of Mevagissey and 1 mile south of Black Head. Small tidal basin with depths of 13 ft. at high water. Protected by pier and breakwater. Dries out over a cable from entrance, and the entrance should not be attempted during onshore winds, or if a swell is running.

MEVAGISSEY

Plan No. 46

High Water —06 h. 07 m. Dover.
Rise 18.3 ft. springs; 14.9 ft. neaps.
Depths *There is 10 ft. M.L.W.S. at entrance, 5 ft. to 8 ft. in the centre of the harbour near the entrance, and 4 ft. farther in. The inner harbour dries out from 3 ft. to 8 ft. and more in certain parts.*

MEVAGISSEY is a pretty Cornish fishing village, with an outer and an inner drying harbour. The outer harbour is well sheltered by the land from prevailing winds from S.S.W. to N.W. The northern pier protects it from the north except in very rough weather, but winds from any easterly direction bring in a swell. It is a bad harbour in strong onshore winds and gales, when shelter can only be found in the inner harbour, which dries out.

Approach and Entrance The harbour is situated at the south side of Mevagissey Bay, a mile north of the low Chapel Point, 3½ miles north of the precipitous

143.   *Entrance to Mevagissey harbour. There are rocks off the northern pier.*

Dodman Point, and 2 miles south of Black Head. The Gwineas (26 ft. high) and Yaw (dries 3 ft.) rocks lie south-west of Chapel Point, and are marked by a red can bell buoy, some 2 cables S.S.E. of the Yaw. The entrance is easy in moderate weather, but it is only 150 ft. wide, and there are rocks off the northern arm of the pier and a strong backwash when a swell is running. It should not be attempted in strong onshore winds.

Anchorage Anchor in outer harbour in 6 ft. or 7 ft. inside the pier, if room can be found and providing the wind is not on-shore. In selecting position anchor

144.   *Mevagissey harbour.* [*Photo: Aero Pictorial*]

145.   *Mevagissey outer harbour. The yacht on left is anchored correctly on north side; the yacht on right is anchored fore and aft between the rocks on that side and the fairway which must be left clear.*

clear of the moorings and do not obstruct the fairway, which is in constant use by fishing vessels. The best position is on north side of fairway, but in light weather there is just room on the south side with anchor fore and aft to prevent swinging on the rocks or into the fairway. The Harbour Master will give directions. With easterly winds the swell enters and vessels which can take the ground will find shelter within the inner harbour, drying alongside one of the quays, if there is room.

Light Gp. Fl. (2) 10 sec. 30 ft. from lighthouse at end of pier. Vis. 10 M. Fog diaphone ev. 30 sec. Occasional.

Facilities Water at quay, and at tap near post above the public lavatory on north side of inner harbour. Diesel oil, petrol etc. at Marine Garage at inner harbour. Several small hotels and many shops. Early closing day, Thursday. Buses to St. Austell, where there is a station. Boat-builder at Mevagissey, also good yacht builder at Portmellon, ½ mile southwards. C.G. and storm signals.

PORTMELLON

THIS little bay, ½ mile south of Mevagissey, provides a good, though rather narrow, temporary anchorage between the headlands. It is pretty and may be used during offshore winds in settled weather, taking soundings to find best position. There is a good yacht builder (G. P. Mitchell) in the cove, and yachts are launched over the sea wall.

PORTSCATHO

A SMALL drying harbour on the west side of Gerrans Bay, situated about 3 miles north-east of St. Anthony Head. It has a steep slip suitable for launching boats about 1½ hrs. each side of H.W. During offshore winds and settled weather there is a temporary anchorage outside.

FALMOUTH

146. *Black Rock beacon*

High Water —06 *h.* 07 *m. Dover.*
Rise 17.2 *ft. springs;* 13.8 *ft. neaps.*
Depths *The eastern entrance channel has 7 fathoms M.L.W.S., and the western over 3 fathoms; Black Rock lies between the two and uncovers at half tide. The main channel River Fal is deep as far as Ruan Creek.*

FALMOUTH, the historic Cornish port, is the most westerly of the deep-water natural harbours of the south coast. From time immemorial it has been used by sailing ships. The harbour and the neighbouring rivers and creeks provide one of the best centres for day sailing in the south of England. Falmouth itself is primarily a commercial port, equipped with big dry docks, but beyond the docks there is a good anchorage for yachts and first-class facilities of all kinds. On the opposite side (on the eastern arm) just within the harbour entrance is St. Mawes, which offers clean anchorages in beautiful surroundings. It has something of the attraction of Benodet on the Brittany coast. Between the Falmouth and St. Mawes sides of the harbour is the third arm, the northern, which is the River Fal, largest and deepest arm of the three. It forks 5 miles up, the northern creek (Truro River) leading to Truro and the eastern one, Ruan Creek, forming a shallow continuation of the River Fal.

Approach and Entrance The approach to Falmouth from the west or south is soon under the lee of the land in westerly and south-westerly winds after passing the Manacle Rocks. It is also sheltered from the north, though steep seas may be found in the approach during strong winds.

The entrance lies within Falmouth Bay between Pendennis Point on the west and St. Anthony Head on the east. It is a deep, easily navigated entrance, open to the fetch from the English Channel only from S.S.W. to E. by S. The entrance is very rough during onshore gales blowing against an ebb tide, but it is considered to be one of the safest on the south coast.

Approaching from the eastward give the Dodman Point a berth of about 2 miles, to clear the overfalls which, in bad weather, break on the ledges some 3 to 5 fathoms deep. Also keep well away from Nare Head, for there are dangerous rocks (The Whelps, which dry 12 ft.) south-west of the Gull Rock. This rock is very conspicuous, being an islet 125 ft. high, situated just over ½ mile east of Nare Head. Off the next point (Greeb Point) there are several patches with 14 to 16 ft., and here also are overfalls in bad weather over the 2¼ fathom shoal known as 'The Bizzies'. There is a rifle range near Killygerran Head, and red flag is flown inland during firing. Finally, when rounding St. Anthony in bad weather the overfalls over the rocky patches (3 and 3¾ fathoms) can be avoided by keeping 2 miles offshore, before altering course for the entrance.

In the entrance itself the only danger is Black Rock, which, as mentioned above, uncovers at half tide, and has rocky patches 1 cable south and south-east of the rock, with 12 ft. over them at low water. The shoal is marked by a conspicuous black stone beacon, with globe top-mark and by a red buoy on the south-east. Black rock lies a little westward of mid-channel and can be passed on either side, but the main channel is on the eastern one which is the safer during strong onshore winds.

Within the entrance on the western side is the Falmouth Bank (10 to 17 ft.). Two red buoys are moored near the edge of this bank; the first is on the edge of the Governor patch (covered 12 ft.) and the second is a lightbuoy on the western side of the narrows leading to Carrick Road. Big ships leave the West Narrows buoy to port and turn to the westward through the 19 ft. dredged channel if proceeding to Falmouth docks.

After passing Black Rock beacon most yachts can steer direct across Falmouth Bank to the end of the Dock pier, as there is a least depth of 10 ft. M.L.W.S.

On the eastward side lies the St. Mawes Bank (8 to 15 ft.). The black conical Castle light buoy is moored 3 cables off the Carricknath Point (the point on the south of St. Mawes River), and about 2 cables north-east of this is a R.W. can buoy marking the Lugo Rock to the north-east—which is dangerous, as there is only 2 ft. over it at L.W. For details of buoyage within the harbour refer to the chart.

Lights St. Anthony Head. Lt. Occ. 20 sec. 72 ft. White from 295° to 004°, red to 022°, covering Manacles Rocks. White to 172°. *Fog Signal* Nauto. One blast of 3 sec. ev. 20 sec. The Black Rock buoy carries a red light Fl. ev. 4 sec. When entering at night give a good berth to St. Anthony to clear the Shag

Labels on image: ST. ANTHONY HD. · PENDENNIS PT. · CUSTOM HO. QUAY · PRINCE OF WALES PIER · YACHT CLUB

147.   *Falmouth harbour. Air view facing south-east.* [*Photo: Aero Films*]

Rock and leave the Black Rock buoy to port, after which follow lights as shown on chart. A sharp lookout should be kept for unlit buoys, including the Governor and buoys off Falmouth.

Anchorage and Moorings (1) *Outside:* good holding ground, protected from west, suitable for large ships. (2) *Carrick Road* (centre of harbour) and above. This is used by large vessels, but there is a big swell in southerly gales. (3) *St. Mawes Creek.* In offshore winds or settled weather there is a delightful anchorage south-east of St. Mawes harbour in about 8 ft. Soundings should be taken as the depths shoal towards the shore and also in the direction of the harbour. Tide is not strong inshore. Drying berths alongside quay in harbour but not much room. Water, fuel, hotels and shops. Early closing Thursday. Boatbuilders. Yacht club: St. Mawes S.C. Ferries to Falmouth. In bad weather with onshore winds proceed up river round Polvarth Point. (4) *Falmouth,* off the town, temporary anchorage by permission of Harbour Master, but buoy the anchor, as the bottom is foul and there are moorings and chains. (5) *Falmouth.* Between the Prince of Wales pier and the Royal Cornwall Yacht Club clear of the small craft and moorings and of the channel to Penryn. Royal Cornwall Y.C. has five moorings for visiting yachts. (6) *Falmouth.* Temporarily Custom and North quays for provisioning, etc., where there is about 8 ft. water, half flood to half ebb. Fresh water hydrant at North quay and shops at hand. (7) On moorings in deep hole west and south of Restronguet Point; avoid shallow patch at the entrance to creek. (8) *Mylor.* Off dockyard in 6 ft. (9) *St. Just.* Anchorage during north and east winds in 6 ft., just inside point. (10) There are numerous anchorages in bays and bights in suitable wind conditions (some of which are mentioned below) but keep clear of oyster beds.

The Upper Reaches The upper reaches and creeks of Falmouth harbour offer interesting day sailing but a large scale chart such as Imray, Laurie, Norie & Wilson's Chart No. Y.54, or the large scale Admiralty Chart No. 32 is essential. At H.W. it is possible to navigate as far as Truro where there is a quay, but at low water the river dries out above Malpas off which there is an anchorage. On the western side of the main Fal channel are Mylor Creek (3 ft. in entrance and 6 ft. in pool) and Restronguet creek (dries out except for deep hole inside entrance). Yacht club: Restronguet S.C. On the eastern side is St. Just creek with 9 ft. in entrance, 6 ft. in anchorage, but which dries opposite the church. Ruan creek, which is the eastern fork of the River Fal joining Truro River, is navigable for a short distance and offers a good anchorage within its entrance.

The Penryn creek above Falmouth is dredged to 10 ft. and buoyed for ½ mile above Greenbank at Falmouth, as far as Boyers Cellars, and at high water

148.   *St. Mawes.
The anchorage is to
the right hand of the
outer white yacht.
The picture faces
eastward and also
shows the Porthcuel
river winding round
Polvarth Point.
[Photo: Aero
Pictorial]*

is navigable up to Penryn where there are quays and facilities.

Facilities at Falmouth Water from North quay, from Flushing quay or (by permission) from the yacht club. Petrol and oil, T.V.O. and Diesel from pumps at North Quay. Both water and fuel available from pontoon between Y.C. and P.O.W. pier. Excellent shops including yacht chandlers. Early closing Wednesday or Thursday. Many hotels, of which the Greenbank is convenient to the anchorage. Yacht builders and repairers, including Falmouth Boat Construction Ltd., which has a large chandlery. Yacht clubs: R. Cornwall Y.C., Flushing S.C. Customs. Railway station. Buses to all parts. Ferries to Flushing and St. Mawes.

Launching Sites in Falmouth Harbour (1) At Falmouth, Grove Place Dinghy Park, in south-west corner of harbour. Launching hard accessible at all times except lowest spring tides for vessels up to about 30 ft. long. Car park immediately adjacent. Changing and store rooms available at dinghy park. (2) At St. Mawes, slipway at the harbour, which dries out. (3) Up the river at Porthcuel on east side of river, where road runs to slipway and beach. (4) At Mylor adjacent to the dockyard, car park. (5) Also at Mylor Bridge at end of creek, 1 hr. each side of H.W. (6) At Trenewith, south side of Restronguet creek, road terminates at hard by sailing club.

Plan No. 50

High Water —06 h. 13 m. *Dover.*
Rise 17.2 ft. *springs;* 13.8 ft. *neaps.*
Depths *Deep water in the approach; about 9 ft. on the bar, a mile inside the river. Beyond Navas creek the river soon shallows and the bottom is uneven.*

HELFORD RIVER is very beautiful, and is one of the favourite yachting resorts of the West Country. The entrance is simple, and the depth of water adequate for most small yachts. It is protected from the prevailing westerly and south-westerly winds, and conversely it is exposed to the east. Helford River and its various creeks offer a splendid expanse of water at high tide for exploring in a dinghy and for picnics.

Approach and Entrance When coming from Falmouth keep on or E. of a stern transit with the conspicuous Observatory tower at Falmouth on with Pennance Point until Bosahan Point (on south side of river) is well open of Mawnan Shear (on north side of entrance). This will clear the dangerous Gedges Rocks, which lie between Mawnan Shear and Rosemullion Head on north-east of entrance, and which are sometimes marked by a conical black buoy.

From the eastward keep in centre of entrance, but before approaching Bosahan Point give a good berth to the Voose rocks, formerly marked by a beacon, some 4 cables eastward of Bosahan Point. Proceed through the 'narrows' and then avoid the bank marked by a black buoy on the north side of the river opposite Helford creek itself.

The leading marks up the river as far as Navas creek were a white cottage in a group of buildings at Lower Calamansac which should be kept just open of the wooded point at Lower Calamansac. Entry is not diffi-cult, even if these marks are not located, by keeping on the south side of the river off the ledges and leaving the black buoy, mentioned above, to starboard.

When approaching from the west and south keep well clear of Nare Point and Dennis Head.

Lights None.

Anchorage and Moorings (1) Off Durgan any-where in 8 to 12 ft., exposed in easterly. (2) Off Hel-ford. Excellent moorings of Helford R.S.C. or yacht yard on buoys marked for visitors, with moderate dues payable at shop at Helford Point. Or anchor if room in 9

149.   *White cottage (indicated by arrow) just open of the wooded point at Lower Calamansac leads up the Helford River.*

to 30 ft. Strong tide. The mud south is very steep-to in places. Avoid cable crossing river near Bosahan Point, position marked by beacon on each side. (3) On moorings, if any available, inside Navas creek in 5 ft.—note bar at river entrance. (4)On north side of river south of the bar and oyster buoys off entrance to Navas creek. There are oyster beds in Navas creek and off and west of its entrance and elsewhere, on which vessels must not anchor or ground. (5) In settled weather and offshore winds, in Gillan harbour, in 5 ft.—poor holding ground and watch out for submerged rock in the middle of entrance.

Facilities Yacht club: Helford River Sailing Club. At Helford there is a landing place at Helford Point (west of the creek), where water may be obtained from a tap at the shop which sells oilskins, clothes and other things. Boat builders and boats for hire. It is a short walk from Helford Point to the village, where there is a P.O. and shop; provisions and petrol may be obtained. Early closing Tuesday. Launching site at Helford village on south shore, where road crosses end of creek, at 1 hr. each side of H.W.

A ferry for pedestrians crosses the river from Helford Point to the Ferry Boat Inn at Helford Passage on the north side of the river, which is a hotel with restaurant. On this side of the river water may be obtained from a tap at cliff, 200 yds. east of entrance to Navas creek and also at Durgan. Buses to Falmouth from top of hill at Trebah, north of Durgan. Boatbuilders and repairers at Helford and Porth Navas. Launching site at Helford Passage where road runs to water's edge by inn. Car park belongs to the inn. At Porth Navas there is dinghy landing, club, bar, shop, water, fuel and minor repairs.

150.   *Porth Navas creek*

151.   *Helford village.*

Plan No. 51

High Water +06 h. 06 m. Dover.
Rise 18.2 ft. springs; 15.8 ft. neaps.

COVERACK COVE lies about 5 miles north-east of the Lizard, midway between Black-Head and Lowland Point. The dangers in the approach are The Guthens which lie off Chynbals Point for a distance of 1 to 2 cables and cover at high water. On the northward side of the cove there are ledges and rocks off Lowland Point and the dangerous Manacle Rocks which lie between Lowland Point and the buoy marking them.

On the south side of the cove there is a small harbour, which is formed between the land and the pier, leaving an entrance 70 ft. wide. The harbour dries out completely but at M.H.W.S. it has depths of about 12 ft. The cove is sheltered from west and south-west and during offshore winds it offers an interesting anchorage, in settled weather. Coasters usually anchor with the end of the pier bearing about 255° in about 4 fathoms but yachts can get nearer the harbour.

Facilities Garage, hotel and shops. Early closing Tuesday.

Plan No. 52

THIS little harbour lies at the head of Mullion Cove, some 5 miles north-west of the Lizard. It is formed by

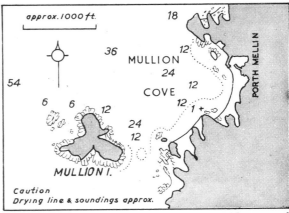

Sketch chart based on British Admiralty Chart No. 777 and with the permission of the Controller of H.M. Stationery Office and of the Hydrographer of the Navy.

two breakwaters, between which is the narrow entrance. The harbour dries out but could be used by berthing alongside the breakwater or quay, but only in exceptionally settled weather, with offshore winds. The cove and harbour are exposed to winds from all westerly directions, and, as even swell from the west causes a surge within the harbour, it would be an awkward place to be caught out in by a change in the weather. The narrow entrance is obstructed at each side by broken masonry at the ends of the breakwaters.

The anchorage in the cove is safer, provided it is used only in settled weather and offshore winds. It is open to the Atlantic from the west, and should be left immediately if the wind shifts or a shift is forecast to that direction. Anchorage is found northward of Mullion Island, in 10 fathoms, but a handy yacht or one with auxiliary power can proceed into the cove itself, taking soundings and bringing up in 2 fathoms with the end of the harbour breakwater bearing approximately east. The bottom is sand and rock, the sandier parts lying rather on the north side of the cove. This anchorage is partly sheltered from the south-west by Mullion Island, but there is a gap open to the sea between the island and the shore.

There is a café at Port Mullion where some provisions may be obtained. Road leads to steep beach where launching possible at H.W. Car park. There are shops, a garage and 'pub' at Mullion village, situated at the end of a rather uninspiring uphill walk of a mile from the pretty little cove. Early closing Wednesday.

152.   *Mullion. Rounding Mullion Island. The cove is off the dip in the hills. Note the conspicuous hotel on the north side of cove.*

153.   *Anchorage in Mullion Cove is better northward of the position shown.*

PORTHLEVEN

Plan No. 53

High Water +05 *h.* 56 *m. Dover.*
Rise 17.7 *ft. springs;* 13.9 *ft. neaps.*
Depths *The entrance* 8 *ft. in centre, north-west off pier but dries out above the lifeboat house.*

THIS small tidal harbour is situated 8½ miles north-west of the Lizard and may be located by a clock tower, a flagstaff and the white houses in the background which are conspicuous from a considerable distance. The approach and entrance are open to the west and south. The port used to be entered by coasters but this trade has almost ceased and it appears to be used by a few small fishing vessels only. Porthleven is rarely visited by yachts. It provides only drying berths alongside the quay in the inner harbour.

Approach and Entrance The entrance lies between the end of the pier on the south-east side and the Deazle Rocks on the north-west side. It is considered a difficult entrance because it is only 200 ft. wide and the Deazle Rocks are not marked by buoys or beacons, nor are there clear leading marks to lead up the centre of the entrance. Pilotage used to be compulsory and it would be un-

154.   *Porthleven, from end of the pier.*

155.   *The entrance to the inner harbour.*

156.   *Porthleven, the entrance at low water.* [*Photo: Aero Pictorial*]

desirable for a stranger to attempt the entrance without local advice except under particularly favourable conditions. There is still a coastguard station but no pilot.

Entrance should be made on a course parallel with the pier, but about 60 ft. west of it. There are ledges of rock extending about 50 yds. or more off the pier end. The approach thus lies between these rocks on the east side and the Deazle Rocks on the west. There is 8 ft. M.L.W.S. at the entrance but it soon shallows. Fishing boats will be seen on moorings in the centre of the outer harbour but they nearly dry out at low water spring tides. Fishing boats proceed in and out of the harbour at fairly frequent intervals and assistance may usually be obtained from the fishermen. When the harbour is closed this is indicated by the hoisting of a red ball on the flagpole at the inner end of the pier; at night when the harbour is closed the two red lights are not shown.

Lights There is an occasional red fixed light 33 ft. elevation which is situated about 100 ft. from the pier end. A second red light has been placed on the east side of the harbour and the two in line indicate the general line of approach, though the distant light should be kept just open to the west of the front one to clear the rocks off the pier end. Approach at night would be dangerous for strangers.

Harbour The outer harbour has wide ledges of rock on the north-west side and the pier on the south-east side but there are rocks at the foot of the pier in parts. The outer harbour dries 5 ft. to 6 ft. The inner harbour lies between the inner pier heads, and the entrance can be closed with baulks of timber in bad weather. The inner harbour dries out completely but there are berths alongside the quay where yachts can lie and depths of about 10 to 11 ft. in the deepest berth at high water springs.

Facilities Water, petrol and some stores. Early closing Wednesday. Boatbuilders. Two small hotels. Good bus service to Penzance and Falmouth and district.

Launching Facilities There is a slipway at the head of the inner harbour which is quite convenient for launching small craft by hand near H.W.

ST. MICHAEL'S MOUNT

Plan No. 54

High Water +05 *h.* 50 *m. Dover.*
Rise 17.7 *ft. springs;* 13.9 *ft. neaps.*
Depths *The harbour dries out but there is about* 11 *ft. at M.H.W.S.*

ST. MICHAEL'S MOUNT is conspicuous from seaward. There is a small drying harbour at the north end which is formed between two piers and there is anchorage to the westward of the entrance.

Approach and Entrance Approach may be made on the large scale Admiralty chart from the direction of the Gear Rock beacon off Penzance steering on the line to the north end of the harbour breakwater at 074°. The principal dangers in the approach are the Hogus Rocks which form a large expanse of reef to the north-west of the harbour, and the Outer Penzeath rock, with less than 6 ft. M.L.W.S., which lies about 3 cables W.S.W. of the Hogus Rocks. These dangers are left to port, and to starboard there is a rock 9 ft. covered M.L.W.S. Nearly a cable S.S.W. of the Mount lies the Maltman Rock which dries 1 ft. M.L.W.S., but this does not interfere with the approach

157. *Anchorage at St. Michael's Mount. It is better to anchor farther northward in line with the end of the breakwater.*

158. *The harbour at St. Michael's Mount.*

from the direction of Penzance. These rocks have no beacons to mark them and some yachtsmen consider that the harbour should not be attempted by a stranger without the aid of a pilot. However, in light weather with a leading wind and an accurate compass the approach can be made with due caution.

The approach gradually shelves from 27 ft. to 9 ft. a cable west of the entrance. Depths then rapidly fall to 2 ft. and the bottom dries out on a line roughly northward of the west pier.

Lights The division of the red and white sectors of Penzance south pier light leads south of the dangers to the northward and a little south of the entrance to St. Michael's harbour, but there are no lights at the harbour.

Harbour and Anchorage There is a pleasant anchorage in 9 ft. about a cable west magnetic of the northern end of the west pier, which can be used in settled weather and offshore winds. The entrance to the harbour is 100 ft. wide and it dries from 5 to 9 ft. There is a Harbour Master who will direct a visiting yacht to a berth alongside the quay.

Facilities There are no facilities on the island except water but all facilities at Marazion, ½ mile to the northward. This can be reached across the causeway at L.W. or by dinghy at H.W. Water, petrol, hotels, banks, shops. Early closing Wednesday but some shops open on all days. Yacht clubs: Mount's Bay S.C. Facilities for dinghy racing. Launching site: at the west end of Marazion on beach, with car park and garage adjacent. Frequent bus services.

Plan No. 55

High Water $+$05 *h.* 50 *m. Dover.*
Rise 17.7 *ft. springs;* 13.9 *ft. neaps.*
Depths *There is about 8 ft. up to and just within the South pier. The outer harbour and area near North pier dries out M.L.W.S. leaving a channel near the South pier 3 ft. except for a shoal about 150 ft. N.E. of South lock gate. There is usually not less than 14 ft. of water in the inner basin, which is open for about 2 hrs. before to H.W.*

PENZANCE is a commercial harbour but it is increasingly used by yachts. It is a useful port of departure for Ireland, the Irish Sea and the Scillies. In strong winds and gales from the south and especially from south-east it is dangerous to run for shelter at Penzance owing to the shoaling water in the approach and because the lock gates cannot always be opened. Mount's Bay is very exposed to winds from this quarter.

Approach and Entrance Penzance lies in the north-western corner of Mount's Bay some 15½ miles north-west of the Lizard. A yacht coming from the eastward should keep 2 to 3 miles off the Lizard to avoid the overfalls and should not stand into Mount's Bay in rough weather until the Boa overfalls have been

159.   *Penzance at high water showing inner basin on right.* [*Photo: Aero Pictorial Ltd*]

passed. On nearer approach to Penzance Bay there are shoals to the southward of Cudden Point which may be avoided by keeping west of the transit of the tower on St. Michael's Mount and Ludgvan church at 341°.

From the westward after passing the Runnelstone follow up the coast keeping a mile offshore as far as St. Clements Island. Between this island and Penzance there are the following dangers: Low Lee rock (marked by R. & W. chequered buoy), Carn Base (unmarked), Gear Rock (marked by a black beacon surmounted by a cage, to be given a good berth) and the Battery rocks to the south-west of the south pier. Steer for the south pier lighthouse at 350° to leave these dangers to port and leave to starboard a wreck marked by a green wreck buoy. Then round in towards the pierheads. Note that at low water springs there is only 8 ft. east of the south pier and see 'depths' for water within harbour. Half a mile north-east of the entrance lie the Cressar Rocks marked by a black and white beacon.

Lights Penzance south pier lighthouse has a light Gp. Occ. (2) W.R. 15 sec. Approach in the white sector. The red sectors on each side cover the outlying dangers,

160.   *Photograph from south pier showing entrance to inner basin on left and the outer drying harbour on right.*

but the western edge of the white sector cuts Gear Rock pretty close.

Tidal Signals from flagstaff on south pierhead. 15 ft. water or over at pier head: day, a ball; night, red light. *Dock gates open:* day, two balls, horizontal; night, two red lights vertical. *Dock gates closed or not to open:* day, two balls vertical; night, red light over green light. When the dock gates are open a green light is shown from north dockhead, and a red from south dockhead.

Anchorage The large outer harbour on the north side dries out at low tide, and is not suitable for yachts. These should use the inner basin, where there is usually about 14 ft. of water. As mentioned above, the dock gates open from 2 hrs. before H.W to H.W. In strong southerly gales the seas break over the south pier, so the north pier is the better for shelter, although here there is often coal dust.

Waiting for tide, anchor outside about 2 cables south-east of the south pierhead, weather permitting.

Facilities Water at quay. Many hotels, restaurants, shops of all kinds. Early closing day, Wednesday. Yacht club: Penzance S.C. Launching site: dinghies may use the slipway at the outer harbour approximately from 3½ hrs. before to 3½ hrs. after H.W. Two boat yards; scrubbing at hard in outer harbour. Station and buses to all districts. Passenger service to Scilly Isles.

Plan No. 56

High Water +05 h. 50 m. Dover.
Rise 17.7 ft. springs; 13.9 ft. neaps.
Depths *The entrance has been dredged to 13 ft. M.L.W.S., and for about 140 yds. vessels drawing 11 ft. can lie alongside the north pier. The harbour shallows progressively farther northwards, with 6 ft. at the third tier and drying at the end.*

NEWLYN is stated to be better than Penzance as a harbour of refuge when running for shelter, though southerly and S.E. winds bring in a heavy swell outside. It is inconvenient for yachts not equipped with legs, as it is a busy fishing port with limited room to lie afloat alongside the quay. The Harbour Master always endeavours to find a place for a visiting yacht free from disturbance by other vessels, but this is not always possible during the pilchard season in June, July and August. Then the harbour has to accommodate fishing vessels from Looe, Mevagissey and St. Ives in addition to its own fleet. The south pier has 13 ft. M.L.W.S. at its extremity, but should not be used by yachts as it is reserved for stone ships and commercial vessels.

161. *The spar buoy within the entrance which is left to port.*

162. *Course is altered to starboard. The channel lies between the fish quay to starboard and the edge of the dredged channel to port, in line with two posts with boards on the fish market.*

The best way of visiting Newlyn is to anchor outside in Gwavas Lake and enter the harbour by dinghy.

Approach and Entrance From the southward follow the instructions given for Penzance, but alter course when Newlyn pier heads bear W.N.W., leaving Carn Base well to port. From the north-east give Gear Rock a sufficient berth. Enter between the pierheads, when a small red and white spar buoy will be seen ahead. This marks the end of the new slipway, and course should be altered to starboard to leave the buoy to port. The west side of the harbour dries out, but there is a dredged channel for about a cable on the east side parallel with the north pier. The west side of this dredged channel is marked by the transit of two red and white leading boards on posts situated on the fish market.

Lights South pier lighthouse: light Fl. W. 5 sec. 9 M. 253° to 336° Nauto (occasl.). North pier: fixed red 2 M. 238° to 240°, white over harbour. Slipway spar buoy has red and white Scotchlite reflectors. Two red lights are sited on the leading boards marking the west edge of the dredged channel. Also a small red light on inner pier.

Anchorage (1) Outside in Gwavas Lake in offshore winds; east of the south end of the North quay, clear of the fairway in 2 fathoms. Good holding ground and well sheltered from north and west. (2) Lie alongside outer part of north pier in 6 to 11 ft. but apply to Harbour Master for berth, least inconvenienced by

163. *The fish market on which there are two posts with R.W. boards, which in transit mark the west side of the dredged channel.*

Plan No. 57

High Water +05 *h.* 50 *m.*
Rise 17.7 *ft. springs;* 13.9 *ft. neaps.*
Depths *Dries out at L.W. At M.H.W.S. there is about* 16 *ft. and M.H.W.N. about* 12 *ft. Bottom gravel on rock.*

movements of fishing vessels. Legs necessary when not alongside as no room elsewhere to lie afloat.

Facilities Water by hydrants at all berths. Diesel oil hydrants and petrol at Ridges on the quay. Two yacht repairers, J. Peak & Son and H. N. Peak. Slipway up to 90 ft. keel, 11 ft. draft available at reasonable rates on application to Harbour Master.

Three small hotels. All stores. Early closing Wednesday. Frequent buses to Penzance and elsewhere. Station at Penzance. Launching sites: by arrangement with Harbour Master only, as the harbour is in continuous active use by fishing vessels.

MOUSEHOLE HARBOUR is a small drying harbour formed by two breakwaters leaving an entrance only 36 ft. wide. The harbour is well protected except in strong southerly, south-easterly and easterly winds. The harbour entrance can be closed with baulks of timber. The harbour and village are picturesque and much frequented by artists. There is a good anchorage outside during offshore winds.

Approach and Entrance Mousehole is situated 1¼ miles south of Newlyn and lies west of the small St. Clement's Island, which makes it easy to locate. There are rocks on the north, east and south sides of St. Clement's Island, and the harbour should be approached from the southward, following parallel with the line of the Cornish coast, and passing rather west of midway between the shore and St. Clement's

164. *Mousehole harbour at L.W. [Photo: Aero Films]*

Island. Once the island is abeam a detached shoal south-west of it will be cleared, and the water between the island and the harbour is clear of dangers, apart from the rocks fringing the western shore and the seaward side of the breakwater. Depths in the approach are 6 fathoms south-west of St. Clement's Island, 3 fathoms when it is abeam, after which the water shoals rapidly to ¼ fathom off the entrance.

Lights Two white lights are exhibited on the northern pier head, but when the harbour is closed a red light is substituted.

Harbour and Anchorage Yachts dry out alongside the inner sides of the breakwater and the deepest berths are near the entrance. There is a Harbour Master who will give instructions for berthing. The anchorage outside provides good holding ground. It is sheltered by the land from north and west and St. Clement's Island provides partial protection from light east winds, but it is open to south and south-east which are dangerous quarters in unsettled weather. Take soundings to find best position to anchor, approximately midway between the south breakwater and the middle or south of the island.

Facilities Water and petrol. Three small hotels, several shops. Early closing Wednesday. Launching site: slipway in harbour. Car park near by. Buses to Newlyn and Penzance.

165. *The anchorage between Mousehole and St. Clement's Island*

Plan Nos. 58, 59, 60

High Water (*St. Mary's*) +05 h. 51 m. *Dover*.
Rise 16.2 ft. *springs*; 12.4 *neaps*.
Depths *Up to* 12 ft. *in St. Mary's harbour.* 4 ft. *to* 30 ft. *New Grimsby harbour* (*Tresco*).

THESE islands—some forty-seven of them—have a charm that only a personal visit can reveal, they are a 'cocktail' with ingredients from England, Scotland and the tropics.

Only five islands, each so different from the other, are inhabited—St. Mary's, Tresco, St. Martins, Bryher and St. Agnes; of these St. Mary's is the biggest with Hugh Town built around the harbour as its 'capital'.

Any yacht exploring these islands should have the largest scale Admiralty charts aboard (No. 34 for all the area and No. 883 which covers St. Mary's and Crow Sounds on a larger scale). The charm of this archipelago should not lull the navigator into a false sense of security as there are many hidden dangers in the form of pinnacle rocks with strong tidal eddies around them. Local knowledge is very desirable if any

intricate passages between the smaller islands are contemplated. Here only the safest four, of the six, approach channels to St. Mary's Road will be described.

Off-lying Dangers These are numerous and clearly marked in Admiralty chart No. 34. All rise suddenly from the 20-fathom line; mentioned here—only because of their isolation in the extreme west—are the Crim Rocks (6 ft. high) and others near them lying about $1\frac{1}{2}$ miles north of the Bishop Rock. Approach

166.   *Round Island. This island, situated on the north side of the Scillies, is conspicuous by its shape and white lighthouse at its summit.* [*Photo: Aero Films*]

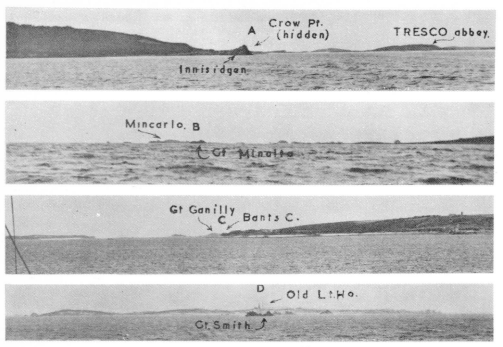

167.
A. Crow Sound. Innisidgen in front of distant Crow Point, Tresco.

168.
B. St. Mary's Sound. Gt. Minalto in front of Mincarlo.

169.
C. Broad Sound. Bant's Carn (St. Mary's) in front of Gt. Ganilly Telegraph Tower. St. Mary's is on right and Crow Rk beacon with distant St. Martin's is on left. Detached distant island is Nornour.

170.
D. North Channel. Gt. Smith rocks in front of old lighthouse on St. Agnes.

into these islands in thick weather is extremely dangerous and the greatest caution is needed if the distant leading marks cannot be seen. If in doubt lay-off, but an approach to Crow Sound from the south-eastwards is the safest providing the bar is not crossed and one anchors to the east of the Hats buoy. At night also, if seeking the lee of the islands, a safety factor is offered by Peninnis light becoming obscured bearing about 231° —as long as this light is visible in a W.S.W. direction the vessel is clear of dangers, unless near the light.

Approach Channels from the East

Crow Sound (view A) The flood tide flows into here, thus the Hats buoy is left to starboard, after which the transit is left and the rock (dries 2 ft.) off Innisidgen Island (22 ft. high) given a clear berth if near L.W. At L.W. there may be much weed over the bar ($\frac{1}{2}$ fathom) but with care a clear channel can be found. As Bar Point is rounded Crow Rock beacon is left to starboard.

St. Mary's Sound (view B) Approach from the south-east to avoid Gilstone. The transit marks may be a little difficult to pick out but there is deep water close to the south of the rocky Peninnis Head with lighthouse (Fl. ev. 15 sec.) set back and a bell buoy marks the Spanish ledges to port. However care should be taken when to the south of Garrison Hill not to get too close to the Woolpack beacon as there is a $1\frac{1}{2}$ ft. patch $\frac{1}{2}$ cable west of it. After leaving the Bartholomew

buoy to port, round slowly to the N.N.E.; deep draft yachts may want to take note of the clearing marks (E1 and E2 on chart) for the Woodcock ledge with $9\frac{1}{2}$ ft. over it.

Approach Channels from the West

Broad Sound (view C) The leading transits are rather far distant and may not be visible. However the channel is buoyed starting with the Flemming ledge to the north of the Bishop Rock lighthouse, after which the Gunners buoy is left to port. Next make for the Old Wreck buoy, leaving it to starboard, but take care to keep clear of the Jeffery Rock (1 fathom) if of deep draft. The leading marks should now be visible and they will take the vessel clear to the south of Spencers Ledge ($1\frac{3}{4}$ fathoms) and the Southward Well (dries 5 ft.) respectively $8\frac{1}{2}$ cables to the S.W. and 4 cables to the S. of Sampson.

North Channel (view D) A cross tide may be experienced in this channel, but given reasonable visibility the leading marks are good. The main danger is Steeple Rock ($\frac{1}{4}$ fathom) on the north side. Keep on the transit until the Broad Sound transit is picked up.

Entrance to St. Mary's Pool and Harbour Once in St. Mary's Road, most yachts will wish to bring up in the pool or harbour. The only danger is the Bacon ledge, or Pool ledge ($\frac{3}{4}$ fathom), which is flanked on the north-east by The Cow which dries. Of the two leading marks illustrated, the southernmost one—

171.   *Hugh Town harbour, St. Mary's.* [*Photo: Aero Films*]

172. *E2. One of the two clearing marks for Woodcock Ledge—the Creeb Rocks in line with right extreme of St. Martin's.*

173. *F. Entrance to Hugh Town harbour—Old Man beacons in line. (Note L.B. slip on right.)*

174. *G. Alternative entrance to Hugh Town harbour—Buzzer Mill in line with Old Smithy (white gable end).*

175. *New Grimsby Sound. H. Leading line—Hangmans I. west side in line with Star Castle on distant St. Mary's.*

view F—is perhaps the more easily distinguished. During February and March white leading lights are shown on the Old Man beacons between six and eight o'clock in the morning and evening.

An Alternative Anchorage If a blow from the south-west is likely, larger yachts which may have brought up in St. Mary's Road would be wise to leave by St. Mary's channel and anchor off Watermill Bay to the north-east of the island.

Facilities Although the smaller inhabited islands have very small village stores, Hugh Town on St. Mary's offers much in the way of mainland facilities such as a Post Office, a chemist, a hospital, provision stores, banks and a few hotels. A limited amount of petrol and fuel oil is available. A bus runs to the airport from which there is a fairly frequent daily air service to Land's End (booking usually required) and a daily steamer service runs each afternoon in the summer to Penzance. Water is available on application to the Harbour Master, and boat building facilities can be obtained from Mr. S. G. Ellis, Mr. T. H. Chudley or the Isle of Scilly S.S. Co.

New Grimsby Harbour—Tresco This island is justly famous for its tropical gardens and many yachts like to bring up in the passage between the island and Bryher. The entrance from the north-west is a little tricky and should only be attempted for the first time in favourable weather conditions, with a leading wind or under engine. Clear of the north-west entrance a flood tide, north-east going, of 2 to 4 knots may be experienced. Keep on the transit (see view H) and give particular attention to the Kettle and Kettle Bottom ledges which dry about a cable to the north-east at the entrance, and also to a drying rock which is inside the entrance but scarcely $\frac{1}{2}$ cable to the north-east. There is a deep anchorage in 30 ft. between

Cromwell's Castle and Hangman Island; after this the bottom rapidly shoals to less than 6 ft. off the quay at New Grimsby on Tresco. The continuation of the passage through into St. Mary's Road (or entrance from it) is possible but only when the height of the tide permits as it has many drying patches and general depths of only a foot or so. A hotel has been built on the island.

176. *A view of Cromwell's Castle, Tresco, with St. Mary's behind and Bryher with Hangman's Island on right.*

177.   *Deal. The all-concrete pier taken from the south. Just south of the pier is 'The Downs'.*

178.   *South Foreland lighthouse. [Photo: Aero Films Ltd]*

PART II

PASSAGE NOTES—PRINCIPAL HEADLANDS

THE tidal streams on the south coast of England provide an important factor in navigation. Tidal charts are not included in this book as the reader is referred to the *Admiralty Pocket Tidal Stream Atlases* which, subject to any increase in price, cost only 4s 6d and last a lifetime. They are issued for the English Channel as a whole, the Solent and the approaches to Portland. Small tidal maps will also be found in *Reed's Nautical Almanac* and the *Yachting World Diary*.

What is perhaps more important to the coastal navigator is the time of change in the direction of the tidal streams for principal headlands. The tidal constants appearing below are in reference to H.W. Dover. The spring rates are also given, but the rates vary hour by hour, obtaining their maximum strength at about half tide. The constants have been extracted from *The Channel Pilot* Volume I by kind permission of the Controller of H.M. Stationery Office and of the Hydrographer of the Navy. It is thought that these will prove useful in the summarized form in which they are presented, coupled with the author's notes and supplemented by recognition photographs of the headlands taken by the author, Mr. J. Kentish and others. These notes are arranged from east to west.

North Foreland Conspicuous lighthouse Gp. Fl. (5) W.R. 20 sec. 20 M., 188 ft. elevation on bold, nearly perpendicular chalk cliffs. At position 3.2 miles 141° from headland: north stream —0120 Dover; south-going stream +0440 Dover. Springs 2¾ knots.

The Downs The anchorage off Deal has been used throughout the ages by ships of all kinds seeking shelter from westerly gales. For yachts the anchorage farther north in the Small Downs is better.

South Foreland Bold irregular chalk cliff about 300 ft. high. Two lighthouses on the summit, eastern one disused. Western lighthouse Gp. Fl. (3) ev. 20 sec. 25 M. 374 ft. elevation; Tidal streams between South Foreland and Deal. North —0145 Dover; South +0415 Dover approx., spring rate 2¼ knots.

Dungeness A low promontory with steep beach at its south-east end. Prominent lighthouse. Lt. Fl. ev. 10 sec. 17 M., 130 ft. Fixed R.G. 11 M. same tower 122 ft. E.F. Horn (3) 30 sec. Old lighthouse and nuclear power station adjacent to west. Anchorage in roads on either side of Dungeness according to direction of wind. At position 2.4 M. 140° from Dungeness High lighthouse the east stream begins —0200 Dover. West stream +0430 Dover. Spring rate of about 2 knots.

Beachy Head This is a very prominent chalk headland. About a mile west of the head is the disused lighthouse, a circular white tower 47 ft. high, near the summit of Belle Toute cliff and the series of cliffs known as the Seven Sisters. The lighthouse is situated

179. *Dungeness. New lighthouse. It is now dominated by a conspicuous nuclear powerhouse to the westward.*

on the rocks below Beachy Head which extend seaward, and to the south-east of Beachy Head there are the rocks known as the Head ledge extending some ½ mile from the cliffs. The lighthouse tower has a broad red band. *Light* Gp. Fl (2) 20 sec. 16 M. 103 ft. elevation. *Fog* Explos. (1) 5 min. Seven miles east of Beachy Head are the Royal Sovereign shoals with 14 ft. least water over which there are overfalls. They are marked on the southward by the lightship to be replaced by a light tower.

Beachy Head should be given a berth of 2 miles in heavy weather as there are overfalls and rough water to the southward of it. Two miles south of the lighthouse the streams are east —0520 Dover, spring rate 2.6 knots; west +0015 Dover, spring rate 2 knots.

Selsey Bill and the Owers Selsey Bill is a low sharp point which is difficult to locate if the visibility is poor. There is a conspicuous hotel on the west side of the point. Southward of the Bill there are groups of rocks and ledges between which lie Looe channel and 7 miles south-east of Selsey Bill the Owers light vessel is moored. By keeping south of the light vessel danger is avoided but in clear weather and moderate winds the Looe channel, which is marked by buoys, affords a short cut, with the aid of a reasonably large scale chart. Tidal streams in the Looe channel east +0445 Dover; west —0120 Dover. Rate at springs 2.6 knots but faster between the Malt Owers and the Boulder bank. There are local variations in the directions of the streams. South of the Owers light vessel west stream

180.   *Beachy Head and lighthouse from south-west.* [*Photo: Aero Films*]

—0050 Dover; east stream +0540 Dover; 2½ to 3 knots at springs.

St. Catherine's Point

St. Catherine's Point This point is at the southern extremity of the Isle of Wight and lies comparatively low at the foot of the hill which forms the highest part of the island, nearly 800 ft. above sea level. The lighthouse is an octagonal building from which is exhibited a light, Fl. ev. 5 sec., vis. 17 M. at an elevation of 136 ft. A low subsidiary light is also exhibited; fixed red 099° to 116° showing towards the Needles. Fog Tyfon one blast ev. 45 sec. There is a tide race off St. Catherine's owing to the uneven bottom in strong streams. This can be very rough under wind against tide conditions and should be avoided; it is dangerous in bad weather. The violence of the race varies according to wind, tide and swell and is sometimes rougher or calmer than may be anticipated from the conditions. There are also overfalls to the eastward of St. Catherine's and Dunnose and a number of isolated tide rips which locally may be as rough as St. Catherine's race. Tidal stream between St. Catherine's Point and Dunnose: east +0515 Dover, west −0015 Dover, maximum spring rate 5 knots, weaker seaward.

The Needles Channel The sharp Needles rocks and the lighthouse form a most popular subject for the south coast marine photographer. They are the best known landmark but the rocks themselves are by no means conspicuous from a distance in hazy weather. From the west or south-west it is the high white cliffs above Scratchell's Bay, just S.E. of the Needles which will first be seen, and the high down 3 miles east on which stands Tennyson's Cross. The light on the outer Needles Rock is Gp. Occ. (2) 20 sec. 14 M. elevation 80 ft. Red from 291° to 300°; white to 083°; red to 212°; white to 217°; green to 224°; obscured elsewhere. Fog Tyfon (2) 30 sec. The tidal streams west of the Needles are very strong and in the Needles channel they are stronger still. The main flood which runs north-east from Durlston Head divides as it approaches the Needles and runs north-east into the Needles channel with a strong set towards the Shingles and east to Freshwater Bay. The ebb streams meet off the Needles channel and run towards Durlston Head. In the Needles channel off Hurst Point north-east stream +0505 Dover; south-west stream −0055 Dover, 4 to 5 knots at springs. Off the Needles the streams tend to be earlier.

Immediately off the Needles lighthouse there is a small rock and the remains of a wreck. There are strong overfalls over the Bridge where the bottom is very uneven for nearly a mile as far as the Bridge buoy. There are also overfalls on the ebb tide for a considerable distance westward of the approach and tide rips in the Needles channel and off Hurst Point. Once within the channel there is usually some shelter either from the Isle of Wight or from the Shingles banks on the north side of the fairway. The approach and the channel itself is very rough in westerly, south-westerly and southerly winds, and dangerous in gales from these directions on the ebb tide. Once across the Bridge and

181. *St. Catherine's Point.*

182. *Hurst Castle from south-west showing low light (red tower centre) and high light (white tower background).*

within the Needles channel navigation is straight-forward as the fairway is well marked by buoys but a lookout should be kept for the set of the streams, especially of the set towards the Shingles in the approach.

In heavy weather the approach to the Solent is safer through the north channel which lies to the north of the Shingles. This channel has a least depth of 12 ft. A vessel should steer from Christchurch Ledge buoy approximately E.N.E. towards a prominent white (or cream) house near to shore at Milford on Sea. When the North Channel B.W. buoy (Gp. Fl. 3) is approached leave it to starboard. On arrival off Hurst beach this may then be followed up at a distance of about a cable. The north channel joins the Needles channel between Hurst Point and the spherical red and white North-east Shingles buoy. There are heavy overfalls at this point and vessels should not pass close to Hurst Fort on account of the ridge of sand and gravel which extends southwards from it and is known as the Trap.

The western end of the Isle of Wight should be avoided if possible in strong onshore winds and swell. It is better to make Poole or approach the Solent at the east end of the Isle of Wight under the lee of the land.

Hengistbury Head This headland, 5 miles east of Bournemouth pier and 1 mile south-west of the entrance of Christchurch harbour, is of local importance as it is the only headland between the Needles and Handfast Point and is conspicuous from seaward. It is composed of dark reddish ironstone, but often appears of a yellowish colour from seaward; the shape is shown in the photograph. A stone groyne, marked by an iron post with cage, extends from it a cable southwards, and there are shoals with 4 and 5 ft. over them $\frac{1}{2}$ mile to south-east. Christchurch ledges, with depths of 9 to 19 ft. extend $2\frac{3}{4}$ miles south-east, their extremity being marked by a red can buoy. Tidal streams are strong at springs in the vicinity of the buoy, and there are overfalls on the ebb tide near the buoy and over the ledges. The streams within Christchurch Bay itself are weak.

Peveril Point to St. Alban's Head There are two recognized tidal races within this area, a small but vicious one off Peveril Point and the larger race off St. Alban's Head. There are also local tide rips and under certain conditions rough water may be found practically the whole way from Handfast Point and Old Harry rocks at the entrance of Studland Bay to St. Albans and westward. The reason may be partly due to uneven bottom but principally to the strength of the tidal streams.

Peveril ledges extend about $\frac{1}{4}$ mile from the low Peveril Point on the south side of Swanage Bay. The depths on the ledges gradually deepen seawards and the end of the reefs is marked by a red and white chequered buoy. The tidal streams set straight across the ledges which constitute a danger if a yacht is becalmed. Three cables eastward of Peveril Point the streams are N.N.E. $+0500$ Dover $1\frac{1}{2}$ knots; S.S.W.

183. *The Needles from north-west, with the white cliffs over Scratchell's Bay and Sun Corner in background. These chalk cliffs are conspicuous for a great distance.*

184. *Hengistbury Head and breakwater from south-east.*

—0215 Dover, 3 knots. In bad weather the race extends from the point to seaward of the buoy and especially to the south-east of it during the west-going stream. On a spring ebb tide the rate probably considerably exceeds the rates given. A yacht running before a strong fair wind at 6 knots will make only slow progress against the stream. In strong south-westerly winds and gales when, having crossed the English channel, a yacht is running for shelter at Poole the seas will be found to be exceptionally rough and broken over the whole area from Anvil Point until she comes under the lee of the land at Swanage Bay to the northward of Peveril Ledge buoy.

Off Durlston Head about a mile E.S.E. the north-east-going stream begins +0530 Dover; S.W. —0030 Dover; 3 knots springs. Durlston Head is a rough headland of a characteristic shape shown in the photograph, and is easily identified by the castellated building on its summit.

Anvil Head, nearly ½ mile to the south-west of Durlston, is easily located by the lighthouse which stands above it. Light. Fl. 10 sec. 18 M. 149 ft. Fog E.F. Horn (3) 30 sec. There is a local eddy on this coast running contrary to the main stream outside. The westerly eddy close inshore commences about —0200 Dover and extends along the Dorset coast westward beyond Lulworth. The inshore eddy to the eastward commences about +0500 Dover, quickly becoming strong.

St. Alban's Head is the most southerly on this part of the coast and its shape with cliffs at the summit falling into rocks at the base is easily recognized from the photograph. Off this head there is a considerable tidal race which lies eastward of the head on the flood tide and westward on the ebb. The race varies considerably in its position and its severity. It extends some 3 miles seaward except during southerly winds when it lies closer inshore. It may be avoided by giving the land a berth of 3 miles. Here the easterly stream begins about +0545 Dover; west —0015 Dover, attaining a rate of between 4 and 5 knots at springs. There is a passage of nearly ½ mile between St. Alban's Head and the race, especially during offshore winds. Thus vessels can avoid the worst of the overfalls by keeping into St. Alban's Head where deep water is found close to the shore. The inshore passage has the advantage of the early fair eddy but a local eddy runs down the west side of St. Alban's Head to the south-east nearly continuously. In good weather and in absence of swell the inshore passage avoids the worst of the overfalls although it is not entirely immune from tidal disturbance and varies in width.

Lulworth Gunnery Ranges Gunnery ranges are generally not specified in this book, but the Lulworth ranges extend so far that they merit special attention.

The sea danger area is divided into parts. (a) That which is used intensively for a minimum of five days each week and (b) that which is used less intensively and a maximum of six days in one month. These areas are changed periodically. Times of firing and areas to

185. *Anvil Light and Durlston Point from south-west.*

186. *Handfast Point and Old Harry from north.*

be used are notified to neighbouring Harbour Masters, Coast Guards, and Yacht Clubs.

As a general guide to the areas used the *Intense Area* stretches south from Lulworth Cover for 11,000 yds. then east to a point 2,000 yds. due south of St. Alban's Head. The *Less Intense Area* stretches south from Lulworth Cover for 20,000 yds., then eastward to a point 17,000 yds. due south of St. Alban's Head, then north joining a point 2,000 yds., south of St. Alban's Head. On the six days per month both areas are used simultaneously.

Warning Signals are exhibited on St. Alban's Head and on Bindon Hill to the east of Lulworth Cove, and are read thus:

(Intense Area) *By Day* Red flag and one black ball.

(Intense Area) *By Night* One red light.

(Less Intense Area) *By Day* Red flag and two black balls.

(Less Intense Area) *By Night* Two red lights one above the other.

Normal firing times are between 0830–1700 hrs. daily. No firing takes place on Public Holidays.

Up to date information can be obtained by phoning the range safety officer (Bovington Camp 321 Ext 219).

Portland Bill and Race The Race lies south of Portland Bill, a little to the westward during the ebb and to the eastward during the flood, where in bad weather there is confused and dangerous water so far as and over the whole of the Shambles. The worst part of the Race extends nearly 2 miles from the Bill and it is well defined by the area of overfalls. South of the Race the seas are influenced by the local tidal streams and are disturbed and steep for a considerable distance, especially when the tidal stream is ebbing against westerly and south-westerly winds. In such conditions it is best to give the Bill a berth of at least 3 and preferably 4 miles or more. At spring tides the Race sometimes attains a rate exceeding 5 to 7 knots, but these speeds are not uniform as the streams vary in speed and direction according to the hour of the tide and position. South-west of Portland, during the west-going stream there is a northerly set into West Bay, which at times is strong. Owing to the local variations in the streams within 5 miles or more of Portland, reference should always be made to the Admiralty pocket tidal stream atlas of the 'Approaches to Portland', price at present 4s.

When proceeding past Portland Bill the yachtsman has the alternatives of passing outside clear to the south of the Race, or, if the tides are right, of sailing through the inner passage between the Race and the Bill. Local yachtsmen also use the passage between the Shambles and the Race in good weather by keeping the north-east breakwater lighthouse in line with Grove Point and leaving the West Shambles light buoy 3 to 4 cables to the eastward. This passage is not recommended to strangers, especially at spring tides, owing to the risk of being set into the Race or across the Shambles where there are overfalls and heavy seas during bad weather or swell.

The outside passage presents no difficulty, except

187. *St. Alban's Head from west.*

188. *Portland north-east side.*

189. *Portland Bill from east inside the race, showing beacon right on the end.*

190.   *Golden Cape may be seen from a long distance, even in hazy weather.*

191.   *Beer Head from south-west with Seaton in background.*

for the strength of the stream. About 5 miles south of the Bill the spring rate is about $3\frac{1}{2}$ knots; east $+0545$ Dover; west -0020 Dover.

The inner passage provides a considerable saving in distance, especially between Portland harbour or Weymouth to Bridport, Lyme or Exmouth. The inner passage is a channel about $\frac{1}{4}$ mile wide (varying with direction of wind) which lies between the Bill and the Race. This channel should not be used at night, and even by day only under suitable conditions, for although the water is comparatively smooth, the streams are strong and overfalls are not entirely avoided off Grove Point and west of the Bill, according to wind direction. The correct timing of the passage is a matter of the utmost importance.

When bound westward, round the Bill between 1 hr. before (and no earlier) and 2 hrs. after H.W. Dover. When bound eastward, round the Bill between 4 hrs. after and 5 hrs. before H.W. Dover. Whether bound west or east through the inner passage close with Portland *well to the northward* of the Bill and work southwards with a fair tide to arrive off the Bill at the correct time. For 9 hrs. out of 12 the stream on each side of the Portland sets south past the Bill, towards the Race. On the westward side of the peninsula it sets southwards out of West Bay from 3 hrs. after H.W. Dover, to the following H.W. there. On the eastward side it sets to the south-west from $4\frac{1}{2}$ hrs. before H.W. Dover, to nearly H.W. Dover.

Lights Portland Bill Gp. Fl. (4) 20 sec. 18 M., 141 ft.

elevation, but the flashes change towards north-east and north-west, the changes being from 1 to 4 flashes from $221°$ to $244°$, 4 flashes thence to $117°$ and from 4 to 1 from $117°$ to $141°$; obscured elsewhere on the north side. Diaphone 30 sec. Lower light fixed red, 13 M. over the Shambles $271°$ to $291°$. Shambles light vessel Gp. Fl. (2) 30 sec. 11 M. West Shambles light buoy Gp. Fl. (2) 10 sec.

Golden Cape A useful landmark $3\frac{1}{2}$ miles east of Lyme Regis and 3 miles west of Bridport. The cape rises to Golden Cap, with pronounced yellow cliffs which, with sun on them, may be conspicuous from a long distance even in hazy weather. Inshore streams weak.

Beer Head Inshore streams weak, approximately east $+0600$ Dover; west H.W. Dover. Streams about 3 miles offshore are rotatory and turn about 50 min. earlier, flood first northerly, then through east to south-east, ebb starting south and then turning through west to north-west.

Berry Head Bold limestone headland flat topped, with lighthouse at summit. Steep end falling at about $45°$ to sea. Streams to north $+0540$ Dover; south -0100 Dover. $1\frac{1}{2}$ knots maximum. Light Gp. Fl. (2) 15 sec. 18 M. 191 ft.

Start Point A long sharp-ridged headland with white lighthouse which is unmistakable. There are

192.   *Berry Head from southward.*

193.   *Stàrt Point and rocks from east-north-east.*

194. *Prawle Point and signal station from west-south-west, with Start Point in background.*

195. *Bolt Tail from south-west.*

196. *Bolt Head from south-east with Starhole Bay just showing on right.*

197. (*Above*) *Rame Head from south-east.*

198. (*Left*) *Eddystone lighthouse and stump of old lighthouse.*

rocks off the Start which are awash at H.W. and extend nearly 3 cables south of the Point. The Start race extends nearly a mile seaward of the Point, and its severity depends much on conditions of wind, tide and swell. The overfalls can be avoided in daylight by passing close to the rocks but there is an outlier on the south, so care is needed. It is simpler to give the Point a berth of at least a mile. Three miles southward of the Point the streams are E.N.E. +0455 Dover; W.S.W. −0120 Dover about 2 knots springs. Off Start rocks the streams are about an hour earlier and attain about 4 knots at springs but are irregular at neaps. *Light* Gp. Fl. (3) 10 sec. 20 M. 204 ft. Lower fixed red light 12 M. over Skerries Bank 210° to 255°. Fog siren ev. 60 sec.

Eddystone Rocks This group of nearly a square mile lies 8 miles south of Rame Head, and only covers at H.W. equinoctial springs. They are fairly steep—to except on north-east and south-east. The remains of the old lighthouse stand north-west of the new lighthouse. *Light* Gp. Fl. (2) ev. 10 sec. 17 M. 133 ft. Lower fixed white 15 M. from 112° to 129° over Hands Deep, a bed of sunken rocks 3¼ miles north-west with tide rips which can be dangerous in bad weather. Fog signal: Tyfon (3) 60 sec.

Rame Head to Dodman Point Gribbin Head, about a mile west of Fowey and 7½ miles north-east of Dodman Point, is easily identified by the day mark on its summit. The Cannis Rock lies about 4 cables south-east of it. Streams tend to follow coast. Dodman Head is precipitous, 363 ft., with a stone cross near south-west extremity. Irregular bottom and tide rips 1½ miles seaward.

Lizard Head The Lizard is a bold headland on which are two white towers, of which the eastern is the lighthouse. There is a coastguard station and Lloyd's signal station, which is in almost continuous use with passing ships making their landfalls and departures from the Lizard. Additional features for identification are the hotel on the eastern side of the head and a framework radar mast.

The group of rocks known as Stag Rocks, some of which are above water and others dry 13 ft. to 17 ft., extend about ½ mile south of the Lizard. These can be seen at most states of the tide and avoided, but a mile east of Lizard Head lie the Vrogue Rocks off Bass Point which have less than 6 ft. over them at L.W. The Craggan Rocks, 5 ft. least water, lie north-east of Bass Point, but these dangers will be avoided by vessels proceeding east or west to the southward of the Stag Rocks. The Lizard Race extends 2 to 3 miles seaward of the Stag Rocks, and at times there is a race south-east of the head. The violence of the seas varies considerably according to hour of tide and wind direction, and the seas may be very rough with strong westerly winds against the down channel tide. Under suitable conditions pass outside the Stag Rocks where the streams start east +0145 Dover; west −0345 Dover. Spring rates are 2 and 3 knots respectively and at times stronger. In rough weather or when a swell is running

199.   *Gribbin Head and day mark from south-east. Tywardreath Bay in background.* [*Photo: Aero Films*]

200. . *Dodman Point and stone cross at summit from south-west.*

201.   *St. Anthony Head from south.*

202.   *Lizard Point.* [*Photo: Aero Films*]

especially with wind against a spring tide vessels should keep 3 to 4 miles off Lizard Head.

Lights Lighthouse Fl. 3 sec. 21 M. from 250° through west to 120° Elevation 230 ft. Reflection occasionally seen inshore of bearings. Siren (2) 60 sec. Red fixed light from the high radar mast $5\frac{1}{2}$ cables northeast.

Runnel Stone Situated $3\frac{1}{2}$ miles south-east of Land's End, the Runnel Stone is the outer of two rocks and shoals lying off Gwennap Head, which may be regarded as the westerly end of the south coast of England. It is marked by a red buoy Fl. (2) on the south side and there is no passage for strangers between the buoy and the land, a mile northwards. Streams off the Runnel Stone are variable, approximately east for 3 hrs. from −0600 Dover, west for over 9 hrs. from −0300 Dover. They are strong at spring tides.

Wolf Rock This isolated rock is situated 8 miles south-west of Land's End. It is steep to, and a circular granite lighthouse is built upon it. Light Alt. Fl. W.R. 16 M. 110 ft. Diaphone ev. 30 sec. Tidal streams are rotatory as the Wolf is within the influence of both the main English Channel streams and the streams between Land's End and the Scilly Isles. Tidal charts should be consulted.

203.   *Wolf Rock.*

Ramsgate *Depths* outside entrance 6 ft. on W. side, 4 ft. on E. side. Variable owing to silting and may be less water. 7 ft. alongside W. pier; 8 ft. E. pier. **Traffic Signals** E. pier flagstaff; B. flag (or W. Rev. Lt.) vessel(s) about to enter; onward keep clear. Two B. balls (or R. Rev. Lt.) vessel about to leave; inward may not enter. *Leading Lights* for transit Old Cudd channel 219° 34'. S.W. approach 020° 45'. Range E. pierhead light 4 miles. *Hoverport* moved outside 2 miles W. *Inner Harbour* Lights Qk. Fl. R. at W. and E. sides dock gates. Traffic signals same as at harbour entrance by day. *Night* 2 G. V., enter. One R. over 2 G., leave. Water level Inner Harbour impounded by gates giving 6 to 10 ft. for yachts berthing on E. side in trots alongside East Cross Wall. Marina pontoons on N.E. end.

Sandwich *Hoverport* about 1 mile N. of entrance River Stour. Flight path marked Sph. Or. buoys converging at E. end with Stour approach channel. *At night* 2 Occ. R. Lts. in transit 290° lead up flight path to Hoverport. R. buoy Gp. Fl. (4)10 sec. has been established close to the transit in deep water 1½ miles from Hoverport. No lights Stour channel so anchor S. of buoy and wait for daylight. Marina, yacht club and yard 1 mile below Sandwich with 2 ft. more water than at Town Quay. Swing bridge requires 24 hrs. notice to open.

Dover Entry at the W. entrance permitted for yachts, and this entrance should always be used when feasible. Yachtsmen must obey traffic signals implicitly and also should *request permission* to enter by Aldis lamp or flag signal S.V. to enter, S.W. to leave.

Entrance Signals at W. entrance: *Day* 2 R. balls V., vessels may enter but not leave; 3 R. balls in triangle, vessels may leave but not enter; 3 R. balls V., no entrance or departure. *Night* 3 W. Lts. in triangle, vessels may enter but not leave; 3 R. in triangle, vessels may leave but not enter; 3 R. V., entrance no entry or departure. *E. entrance*: *Day* same as W. entrance. *Night* F. Or. Lt. on N.E. end of detached mole and 2 G. V. S. end of eastern arm. When shown seaward vessels with permission may enter, when shown towards harbour vessels may leave. 3 R. V. no entry or departure.

Signals for Tidal Harbour and Inner Docks: W. letters on B. background at end Prince of Wales operate in conjunction with dock signals. Letter 'W' illuminated, vessels permitted inward through fairway to Wellington dock only and none outward. Letter 'G' illuminated, vessels (other than yachts not allowed to use Granville dock) permitted inward to Granville dock, but none outward. No signal letter illuminated, vessel may pass outwards, not inwards. *Wellington Dock Signals, Day* or *Night* yellow panel illuminated visible to seaward, vessels may enter not leave. Red panel illuminated visible to dock, departure permitted but no entry to tidal harbour or dock. *At Night*, light F.R. at N. and S. pierheads exhibited during tide times and light F.G. each side of dock entrance when a vessel is about to enter or leave. Wellington dock is open from approx. 1 hr. before until just after H.W.

Outer Harbour Yachts should beware Hovercraft fairway, (marked by Sph. Or. buoys) and channel steamers manoeuvring in confined spaces. Instructions for anchoring or finding a mooring will be given by the Harbour Patrol Launch.

Folkestone Ferry Terminal on E. side inner end of breakwater. Commercial traffic increasing. Yachts only welcome for occasional overnight mooring as whole harbour is full up. Corporation taken over inner basin and position may change. *Lights* at S. pier. R. Lt. permits entry, prohibits departure. If eclipsed at intervals caution needed entering. No R. Lt., vessels may not enter.

Rye Rye Fairway R.W. Sph. buoy (Qk. Fl.) established 1.85 m. at 149° from harbour entrance. Steer to this buoy, then alter course to 329° to enter harbour. Foghorn end of E. training wall. 3 lights Fl. R. along W. training wall.

Newhaven Former B. balls for entry signals now Or.

fluorescent. When entering at night keep R. Lt. on Packet Wharf between F.R. and F.G. Lts. on W. and E. piers.

Shoreham Channel to Prince George Lock dredged to 5 not 5½ ft. Range of E. and W. breakwater lights 4 m. Red light radio mast discontinued.

Littlehampton Page 40, 2nd column line 4; B. diamond now W. luminous. *Signals* When black-hulled pilot boat with large white 'P' at bow flies a R.W. flag by day or shows W. over R. Lts. by night, all boats keep clear as a ship is about to enter or leave harbour. If ship signals 1 long and 2 short blasts, keep clear, particularly of narrows at entrance. Fixed bridge, beyond which no vessels with fixed masts can proceed, is being built round the first bend above the swing bridge. On its completion the swing bridge to be removed.

Chichester Harbour The whole harbour including Emsworth Channel is now under one authority. The Harbour Master's office is at Itchenor in the house on right side of the road facing the water. Chichester Fairway buoy has a Qk. Fl. Lt. and West Pole Fl. R. 5 sec. *Lights* established in Chichester Channel Gardner buoy Gp. Fl. (4) R. 10 sec. and N.E. Winner and Wear buoys Gp. Fl. (3) 10 sec. In Emsworth Channel, Marker Point Beacon Gp. Fl. (3) 15 sec. and Sweare

Point Beacon Gp. Fl. (2) R. 15 sec. Local leading lights at Emsworth Qk. Fl. at 020°. At Itchenor shop closed, but Ship Inn supplies ice and if possible helps out with bread and simple requirements. Bus service reduced to a bare minimum.

Langston Harbour Within harbour there is a starboard B. conical N.W. Sinah buoy, Fl. 5 sec., off Sinah Sands and opposite on port hand the E. Milton red can buoy Gp. Fl. (4) R. 10 sec. There are 2 visitors' moorings in deep water for temporary use on E. side of entrance, S. of the cable notices.

Portsmouth On port side of approach channel Outer Spit buoy now Gp. Fl. (4) R. 12 sec., Spit Refuge Gp. Fl. (2) R. 6 sec. Transit for swashway St. Jude's Ch. spire/war memorial 047° 30'. Transit for inner swashway W. side round tower/W. side of conspic. tank 029°. Amendments to *Signals* (5) *Day*. Int. Code Pendant superior to Pendant zero. Keep clear H.M. ship entering, leaving or shifting berth; (6) *Day*. Int. Code Pendant superior to Pendant 9. *Night*. 3 G. Lts. V. H.M. ship under way. Give wide berth. (7) *Day*. Int. Code Pendant superior to Flags N.E. *Night*. G. over R. Lts. Proceed with great caution. Ships (other than car ferries) leaving Camber. (8) *Day*. Flag E. *Night*. R. over amber Lt. Submarine entering or leaving Haslar lake. Light flashes when submarine under way. Keep clear. (9) *Day*. Int. Code Pendant superior to Flag A.

Night. 2 R. Lts. horizontal. Diving boat all round R. Lt. stern and bows. Have divers down.

Anchorages, etc. Camper & Nicholson's marina greatly enlarged. Hardway S.C. welcomes visitors and has 5 visitors' moorings.

Bembridge Harbour Entirely new entrance from N.E. Leave close to starboard beacon Qk. Fl. Or. (with tide gauge), situated about 2 cables W. of St. Helen's Fort. Then follow small buoys, R.W. cheq. to port, B. conical to starboard. Marina facilities at St. Helen's.

Wootton Creek Owing to silting the anchorage in the bight beyond car ferry terminal dries M.L.W.S. but bottom very soft mud. Anchorage outside W. and N.W. of No. 1 beacon in offshore winds.

Cowes Light at the breakwater end on E. side is now Qk. Fl. R. There is a hovercraft channel, marked by fluorescent Or. buoys on the N.E. approach near the Shrape Mud and along E. side of the harbour. Except for 2 pile berths, the visitors' trots at West Cowes have been replaced by the large Cowes Yacht Haven Marina with all facilities. Additional pile moorings have been provided up the river. At East Cowes there is the John Wilment Marina and up the river Medina there is the Wight Marina. A new light Fl. 3 sec. has been established on the W. side of Medina River 1½ cables S. of Folly Inn.

Hamble River Leading light established on white

pole beacon Qk. Fl. R. on Hamble Common (rear) in transit with port-hand pile No. 2 Gp. Occ. (2) 12 sec. (front) at 345½° leads from Hamble Point buoy Gp. Fl. (3) 15 sec. to No. 2 pile. A cable short of No. 2 pile alter course to Rising Sun beacon, on tripod S.W. corner of Rising Sun Hotel, Warsash, Iso. R. 6 sec. (rear) in transit with Warsash Shore B.W. cheq. beacon Qk. Fl. (front) at 024½°. Lights in river have also been established as far as Bursledon Point beacon, Qk. Fl. R. port and Qk. Fl. starboard. Swanwick Marina at Bursledon greatly enlarged. New Mercury Yacht Harbour at Badman Creek (½ mile below Swanwick). Wet berths at Fairey Marine to be added 1973.

Southampton Netley Hospital demolished; only central dome remains. Extensive land reclamation S.W. of King George V dock and construction of container berths with dredged area S. of them.

Beaulieu River Light Qk. Fl. R. on Spit dolphin. Yacht Harbour Marina, Harbour Master's office and all facilities 1 cable above Buckler's Hard jetty.

Yarmouth Harbour Red flag or by night 2 R. Lts. V. on flag pole at N. end ferry jetty indicate harbour full.

Lymington Visitors' moorings in river opposite Town Quay, 5 ft. M.L.W.S. The large Lymington Yacht Haven Marina is entered 2 cables short of the R. Lymington Y.C., leaving Harper's Post, Qk. Fl. R. to starboard. Fortuna dock pontoon added beyond R.L.Y.C. with 52 berths in 6 ft and 20 for shallow craft.

Keyhaven North point of the shingle bank from Hurst High light to the river entrance has moved eastward, and the channel markings near the entrance greatly improved by B.W. starboard hand buoys. Approach with North point of shingle bank bearing about W.N.W. and come onto the leading marks. As the point comes abeam bear sharply to port leaving it close to S. Here the channel is only about 50 ft. wide between the point and a B.W. buoy. Limited anchorage inside entrance.

Christchurch Port-hand buoys now mostly R.W. Sph.

POOLE *Swash Channel* Lights changed. On starboard hand: Poole Bar buoy Qk. Fl. bell. Light on Hook sands No. 13 buoy (opposite Channel buoy) Fl. 3 sec. and on port hand: training bank beacon Qk. Fl. R. Channel buoy Fl. R. 3 sec., South Haven Point now 2 F.R. *Main Channel* Poole Harbour Y.C. Marina constructed E. of Salterns beacon Gp. Fl. (3). Extensive Ferry Terminal development W. of entrance Little Channel to Poole Quays. Beacon Fl. 5 sec. substituted for buoy E. side of Little Channel. Above the bridge 4 ft. M.L.W.S. to Cobbs Quay, where marina-like facilities. Light Qk. Fl. occasional No. 53 starboard buoy at extreme S. of Hamworthy mud flats. *Diver Channel* Leave intersection stake with circular top mark and direction boards indicating Wych and Diver channels close to port as also 'Aunt Betty' No. 54, R.W. Fl. R. 2 sec. (which has been moved further W.). Here bear to port steering 293°, between stakes on either side to join the Main channel at Diver buoy, No. 49 B. conical Fl. 2 sec. *South Deep* starboard-hand buoy at entrance now B. conical.

Weymouth Expunge beacon Fl. in cable area S.E. of S. breakwater. Substitute Bl.W. buoy Qk. Fl. R.

Portland Within harbour, light Qk. Fl. R. 2 cables S. of Sandsfoot Castle and Fl. 2 sec. 3 cables E. by S. of Small Mouth. Many deep-water moorings S.W. corner of harbour, private or Naval Sailing Centre, occasionally available on application.

Exmouth Lights have been added to starboard-hand buoys: No. 1 (Orcombe Ledge) Fl. 3 sec., No. 3 Qk. Fl., No. 7 Fl. 5 sec. which should be left close to starboard. Then follow the F. Or. leading lights at 305° finally bearing to port into the entrance.

Teignmouth The bar shifts so often that no reliable instructions can be given. In 1971 the approach from E. was best, with the white beacon on N. side of the Ness bearing 255°. This gave about 2 ft. M.L.W.S. but it would be safer for strangers to regard it as *drying* 2 ft. M.L.W.S. and approach in fair conditions waiting for sufficient rise of tide and use the echo sounder. Moorings not available off former Morgan Giles yard. Per-

mission sometimes given to berth alongside craft, but best to apply to Harbour Master.

Dartmouth The Kingswear main light is now Iso. 3 sec. W.R.G., R. 317°–325°, W. 325°–336°, G. 336°–343°. Dartmouth shore light now Fl. W.R.G. 2 sec., R. 188°–289°, W. 289°–297°, G. 297° to shore. The white sectors of the lights denote the fairway, which should be adhered to at night, as there are numerous mooring buoys and pot markers each side. Anchorage off Warfleet Cove or below Dittisham Ferry no longer recommended. Yachts may secure fore and aft temporarily to vacant buoys marked D.H.C. before reporting to Harbour Master. No water boat now but water available from hose S. Embankment, apply to Boat Inspector. Fuel for yachts from Marina fuelling pontoon or garages.

Salcombe Lights established for entry at night Sandhill Point Beacon Fl. W.R.G. 2 sec. 7 M., R. 002° 30'–182° 30', G. 182° 30'–357° 30', W. 357° 30'–002° 30'. Approach in W. central sector. When about ½ cable S. of Poundstone come on to leading lights front Fl. W. 1½ sec., rear Fl. W. 3 sec. at 042° 30'. These are situated E. of the Bag and lead up the river to the harbour anchorage.

Plymouth Minor changes in Asia Pass and Drake's Channel. Leave Melampus buoy (S.E. of Drake's Island) Fl. R. 4 sec. port, S. Winter Qk. Fl. starboard, pass between Asia Fl. R. 2 sec. port, Ash (off West Hoe)

Fl. 3 sec. starboard, N. Drake's Fl. R. 4 sec. port, N.W. Drake's Gp. Fl. (2) R. 10 sec. port E. Vanguard Qk. Fl. starboard. Entrance Mill Bay 2 F.R. V. port, F.R. and signals starboard. In Cattewater light Qk. Fl. R. established 2 cables E. of Mount Batten. In Sutton Harbour now 150 pontoon berths with depths up to 6½ ft L.W. ordinary springs. Mostly allocated but limited number of visitors accommodated if room is available: Tel 05 0752–64186. New Mayflower Marina at Ocean Quay, S. point of Mt. Wise, through the Narrows E.N.E. of Cremyll. Deepwater berths for craft up to 70 ft. L.O.A.; 45 visitors' berths.

Falmouth St. Anthony Lighthouse horn 20 sec. Light buoy E.S.E. of Black Rock now Gp. Fl. (4) 15 sec. Vilt B. buoy off St. Mawes Bank in Carrick Road Gp. Fl. (3) 10 sec. and 4 cables N. of it R. can Northbank buoy Fl. R. 4 sec.

Mylor Yacht Harbour consists of a small inner harbour which dries L.A.T., and an area N.E. of it with 220 swinging moorings, with depths ranging from 8 ft. at the outer end down to 3 ft. M.L.W.S. close to the quay. There is about 6 ft. M.L.W.S. in the approach on the leading marks of 3 prominent trees centre of field to right of Mylor Creek with St. Just village dead astern, but strangers best await more water. All facilities near inner harbour.

Isles of Scilly Round Island light Fl. R. 10 sec.

24 M. Siren (4) 60 sec. Occasional lights F.R. on Old Man leading beacons to St. Mary's Pool. If proceeding N. from St. Mary's to New Grimsby leave Nut Rock port, Hulman beacon 75 yds. starboard, Little Rag beacon 75 yds. port. Then steer between Merrick I. and Plumb I. With local knowledge awash M.L.W.S., but strangers best allow drying 2 ft. M.L.W.S. Porth Cressa (S.W. St. Mary's), cable middle of bay, turns S.W. off Penninis Hd., thence across entrance of St. Mary's Sd., then 2 cables S. of Gugh turning N.W., between Gugh and St. Agnes.

PASSAGE NOTES

Royal Sovereign Light Vessel has been withdrawn and replaced by a white tower on white cabin on concrete column, situated 50°.43'.4"N., 0°.26'.1"W. exhibiting Fl. W. 20 sec., 15 M. Dia. (2) 30 sec. distress signals. Helicopter landing platform.

Lulworth Gunnery Ranges Vessels may now pass through Ranges. Passage should be made as quickly as possible. Anchorage, fishing or stopping during gunnery practice prohibited.

Portland Bill and Race Shambles light vessel replaced by lighthouse-buoy, same characteristics.

Radio Beacons These have been regrouped (see *Nautical Almanac*). Further corrections are also given in the *Yachting World* as and when made.

RECONCILIATION WITH CHARTS ON L.A.T. DATUM AND TIDE TABLES

WITH few exceptions the harbour plans in this book are based on datums of approximate M.L.W.S., but the remaining new issue Admiralty charts for the South Coast (some of which have already been published) will become available, all reduced to the lower datum of L.A.T. and with depths in metres. The charted depths on the new issue charts are always *less* than on the older charts where approximate M.L.W.S. datums were adopted for the same area. Conversely in areas covered by the new chart issues on L.A.T. datums the values for rise of the tide and tidal heights in all tide tables (including almanacs or local tide tables derived from Admiralty Tide Tables) will be *greater* than previously.

In order that the depths shown on the harbour plans in this book may be reconciled with the new issue charts on L.A.T. datum and with the Tide Tables the difference between the old and the new datums in feet and tenths has been printed in italics for each harbour listed on the next page. For example, the datum of the chart on which the harbour plan of Portsmouth is based was on the old datum of approximate M.L.W.S., whereas on the new Admiralty chart of L.A.T. datum the tide level at M.L.W.S. is 2.0 ft. above L.A.T. datum, the difference being shown on the list. Thus to reconcile a depth on the harbour plan with the depth on the new chart 2.0 ft. must be subtracted from the depth on the harbour plan. Likewise, 2.0 ft. must be subtracted from the predicted heights in the Portsmouth tide tables to reconcile them with the tidal data in this book, because the heights in the tide tables are measured from a datum which is 2.0 ft. lower than formerly. Thus the rise for Portsmouth is now 15.4 ft., from which deduct 2.0 ft. to give the 13.4. ft. in this book.

Reconciliations for any harbour can be made in the same way, by applying the appropriate deduction printed in italics. Although the differences are shown in tenths of a foot, this degree of accuracy is not required as depths may be considerably influenced by meteorological conditions, especially by the direction of the wind. Predicted heights in some tide tables are already expressed in metres only, so a scale is provided on p. 10 in fathoms, feet and metres.

As already stated, the datums of the older edition charts on which the harbour plans are based were approximately M.L.W.S., but there were a few exceptions as certain of the Admiralty charts were based largely upon older surveys ranging from M.L.W.S. through L.W.O.S.T. to a level occasionally as much as a foot lower. For example the chart of Dartmouth Harbour datum at L.W.O.S.T. as determined in 1900 differed little from the new L.A.T. datum. Again, in charts of harbours such as Richborough on the river Stour or Bembridge, I.W., where the water is impounded by drying sands, the theoretical L.A.T. is never reached, low water being ordinary river level so there is no charted difference between M.L.W.S. and L.A.T.

HARBOUR PLANS AND DATUM DIFFERENCES

Figures in italics denote the difference in feet to be subtracted from depths on each harbour plan to reconcile them with new issue Admiralty charts based on L.A.T. datums

1	Ramsgate	*—0.7 ft.*	21	Lymington	*—1.5 ft.*	40	St. German's *or*		
2	Sandwich	*—0.0 ft.*	22	Keyhaven	*—1.5 ft.*		Lynher River	*—2.1 ft.*
3	Dover	*—2.2 ft.*	23	Christchurch	*—0.0 ft.*	41	Tamar River	*—2.1 ft.*
4	Folkestone	*—2.0 ft.*	24a, b	Poole	*—1.1 ft.*	42	Cattewater	*—2.1 ft.*
5	Rye	*—1.0 ft.*	25	Lulworth Cove	*—1.0 ft.*	43	Looe	*—0.3 ft.*
6	Newhaven	*—0.1 ft.*	26	Weymouth	*—0.7 ft.*	44	Polperro	*—0.5 ft.*
7	Littlehampton	*—0.4 ft.*	27	Portland Harbour	*—0.7 ft.*	45	Fowey	*—0.8 ft.*
8	Shoreham	*—2.3 ft.*	28	Bridport Harbour	*—1.1 ft.*	46	Mevagissey	*—0.4 ft.*
9a, b	Chichester Harbour	*—1.9 ft.*	29	Lyme Regis	*—1.3 ft.*	47	St. Mawes	*—0.4 ft.*
10a, b	Langston Harbour	*—1.9 ft.*	30	Exmouth	*—0.4 ft.*	48–9	Falmouth	*—0.4 ft.*
11	Portsmouth Harbour	*—2.0 ft.*	31	Teignmouth	*—0.3 ft.*	50	Helford River	*—0.4 ft.*
12	Bembridge	*—0.0 ft.*	32	Torquay Harbour	*—2.4 ft.*	51	Coverack	*—0.4 ft.*
13	Wootton Creek	*—2.0 ft.*	33	Brixham Harbour	*—2.4 ft.*	52	Mullion	*—0.3 ft.*
14	Cowes	*—1.9 ft.*	34	Dartmouth	*—0.0 ft.*	53	Porth Leven	*—0.2 ft.*
15	Hamble	*—1.5 ft.*	35	Salcombe	*—1.3 ft.*	54	St. Michael's Mount	*—0.2 ft.*
16	Southampton Water	*—1.6 ft.*	36	River Avon	*—0.0 ft.*	55	Penzance	*—0.2 ft.*
17	Southampton	*—1.6 ft.*	37	River Erme	*—0.0 ft.*	56	Newlyn	*—0.2 ft.*
18	Beaulieu	*—1.5 ft.*	38a, b	Yealm River	*—0.0 ft.*	57	Mousehole	*—0.2 ft.*
19	Newtown	*—1.8 ft.*	39	Plymouth	*—2.1 ft.*	58–60	Isles of Scilly	*—2.1 ft.*
20	Yarmouth	*—1.7 ft.*						

These plans are based upon British Admiralty Charts with the permission of the Controller of H.M. Stationery Office and of the Hydrographer of the Navy

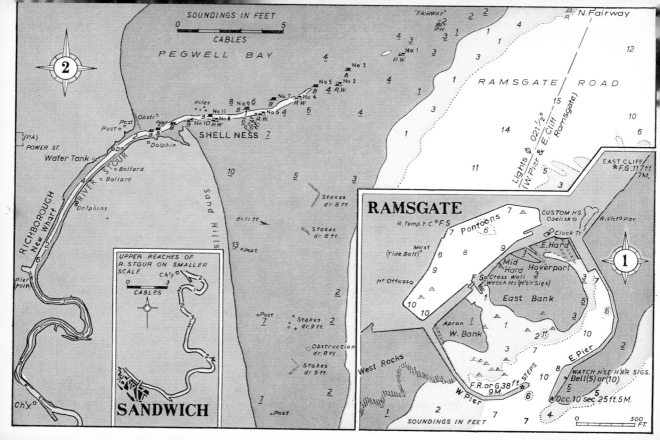

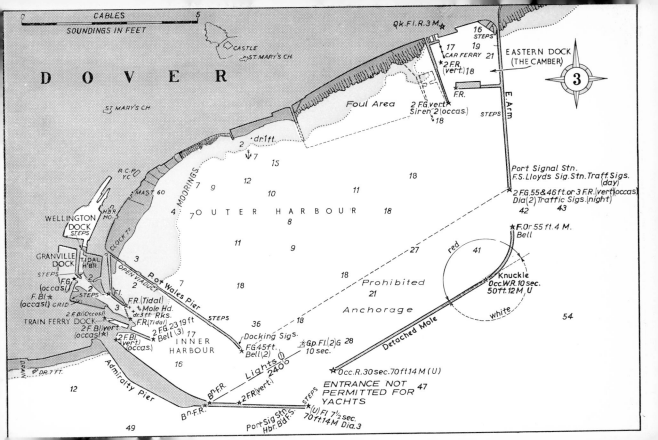

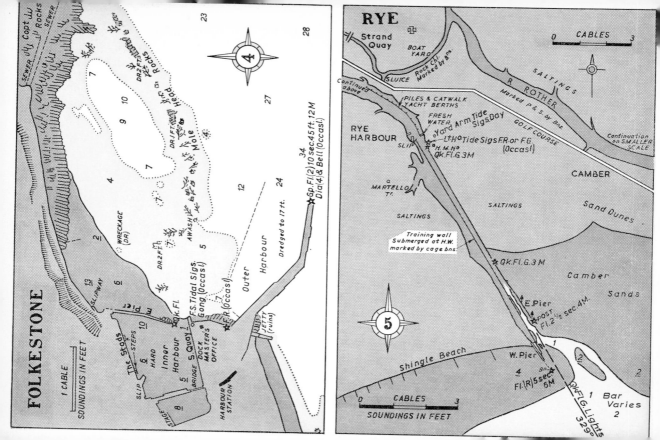

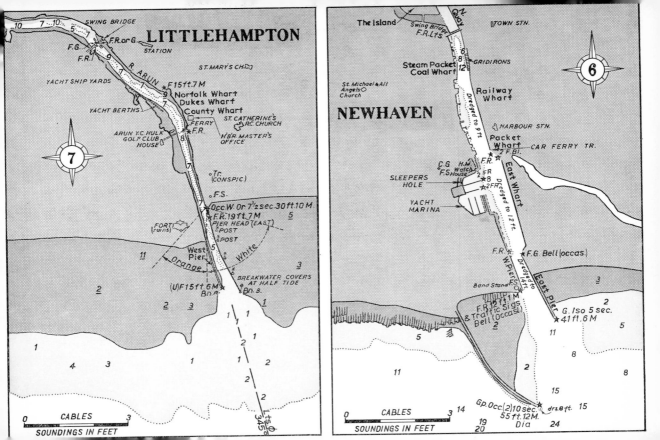

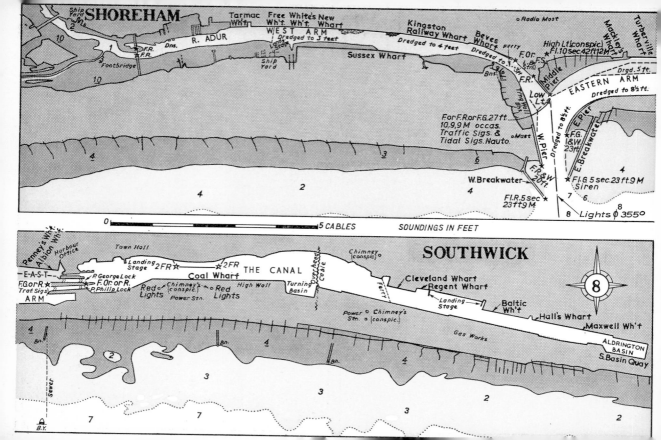

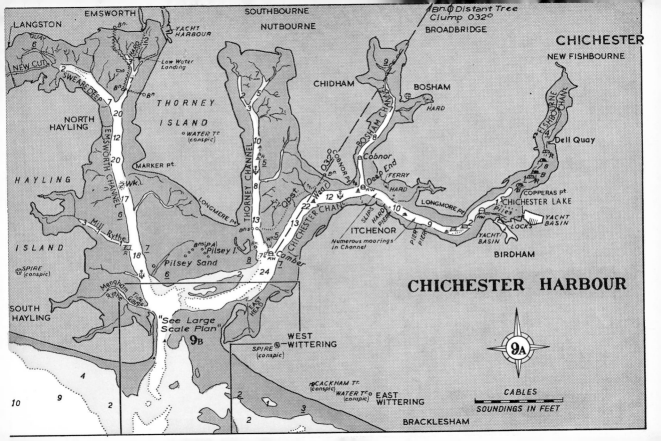

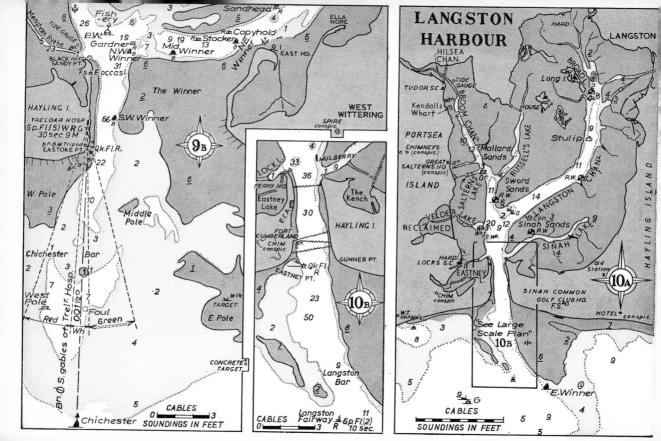

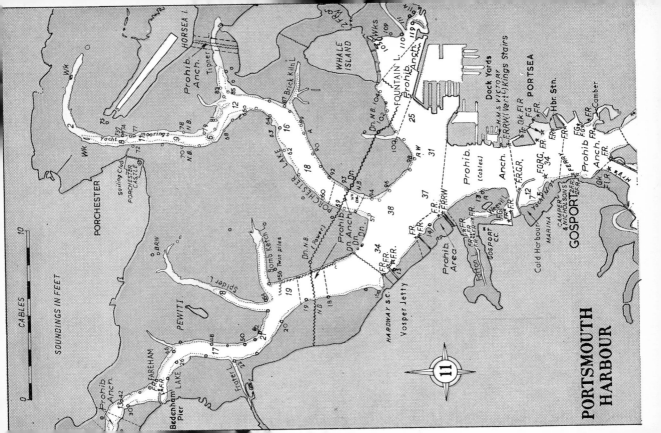

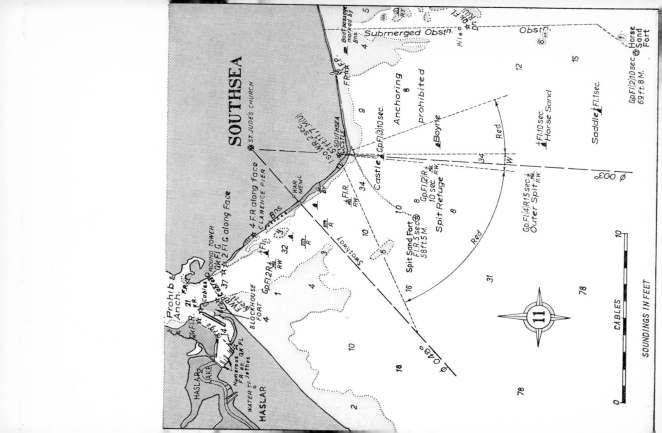

SOUTHSEA

HASLAR

Prohib. Anch.

ROUND TOWER

BLOCKHOUSE FORT

ST. JUDE'S CHURCH
CLARENCE PIER

4 FR along face
2 FR G along Face
4 FR along face

WAR MEM'L

Castle GpFl(3)I0sec.

Spit Sand Fort
Fl.R.5 sec.
58ft.5M.

GpFl(2)R.
I0 sec. RW
Spit Refuge

Boyne

Anchoring
prohibited

Fl.I0 sec.
Horse Sand

Saddle Fl.I sec.

Submerged Obstn.

Obstn.

Horse Sand Fort
GpFl(2)I0sec.
69ft.8M.

GpFl.(4)R I5sec.
Outer Spit RW

SOUNDINGS IN FEET

CABLES

11

0 ... 10

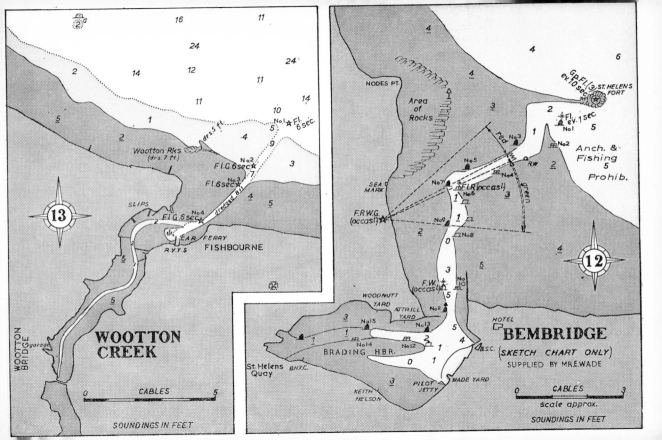

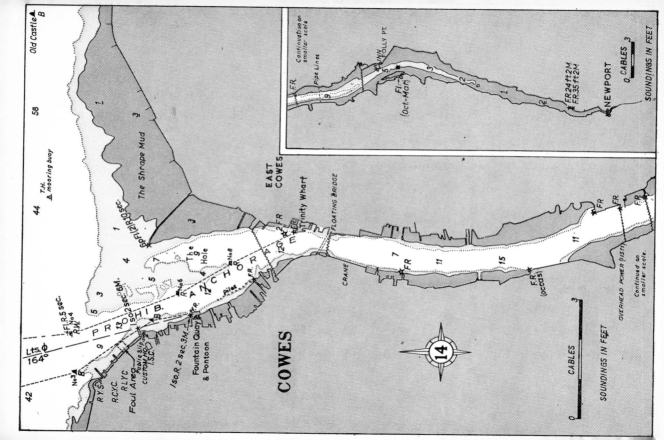

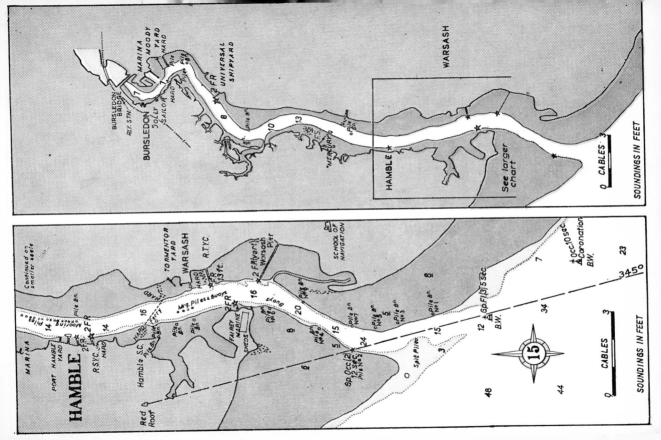

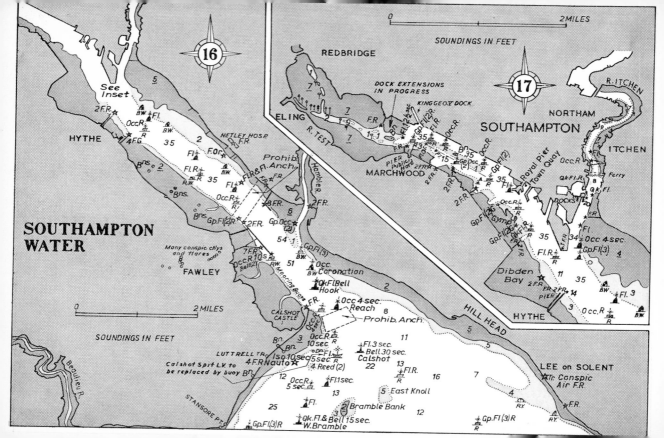

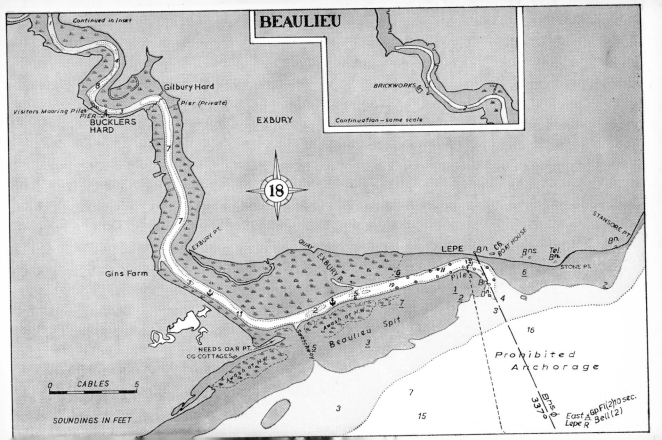

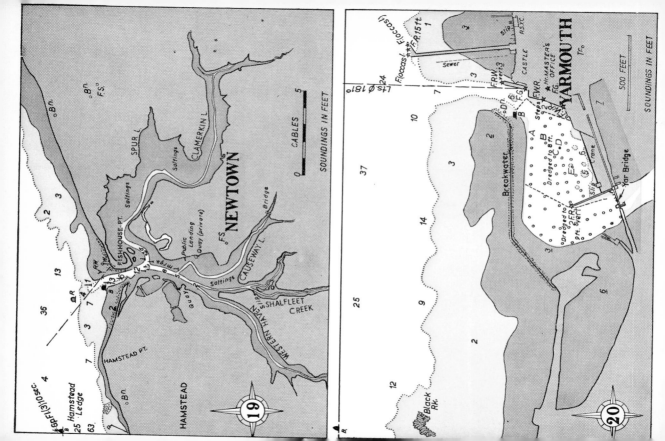

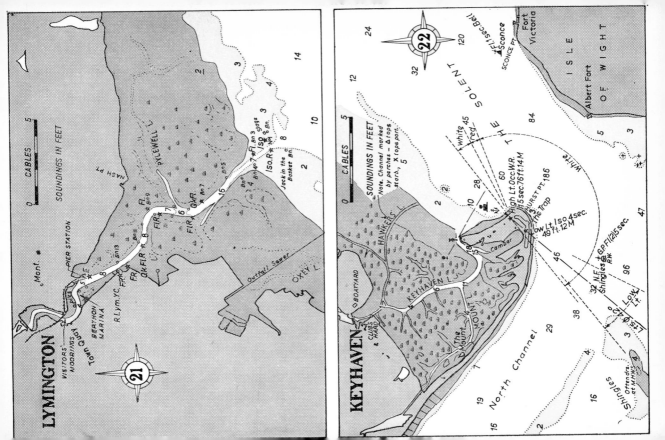

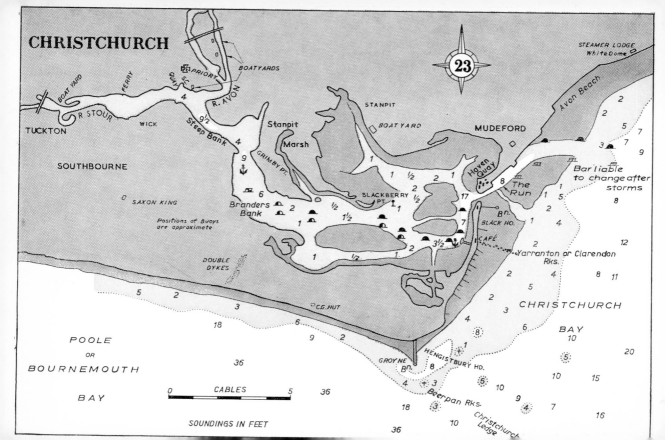

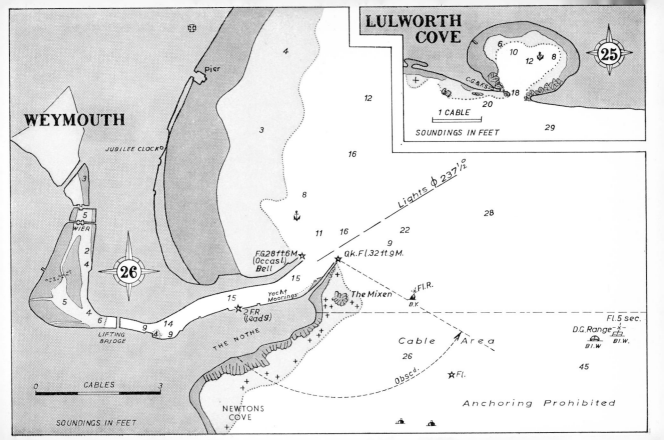

WEYMOUTH

LULWORTH COVE

25

6
10
12 ⚓ 8
C.G.&F.S.
18
20
29

1 CABLE

SOUNDINGS IN FEET

Pier

4

12

3

JUBILEE CLOCKᵈ

16

8

Lights φ 237½°

28

⚓

11   16

22

9

26

Qk.Fl.32ft.9M.

FG28ft6M.
(Occasl.)
Bell

3

5

WIER

2

4

15

Yacht
Moorings

The Mixen

☆Fl.R.

B.Y.

5

15

☆2FR
(leadg)

Fl.5 sec.
D.G.Range—✕—
⊕   ⊞
Bl.W.   Bl.W.

6

9   14

4   9

LIFTING
BRIDGE

THE NOTHE

Cable   Area

26

45

Obscd.

☆Fl.

0   CABLES   3

NEWTONS
COVE

Anchoring Prohibited

SOUNDINGS IN FEET

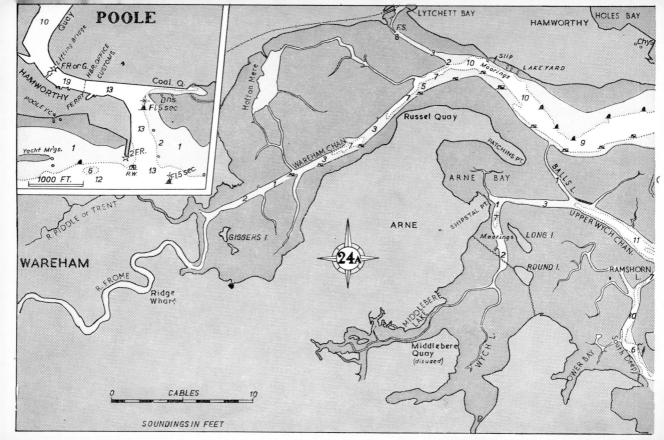

POOLE

HAMWORTHY
HOLES BAY
LYTCHETT BAY
Chy
F.S.
8
Slip
LAKEYARD
10
Moorings
10
7
5
9
Russel Quay
PATCHINS PT.
ARNE BAY
BALLS L.
UPPER WYCH CHAN.
11
ARNE
SHIPSTAL PT.
LONG I.
Moorings
RAMSHORN L.
ROUND I.
WYCH L.
LOWER BAY
SOUTH DEEP
MIDDLEBERE LAKE
Middlebere Quay (disused)

Holton Mere
WAREHAM CHAN.
7
3
GIGGERS I.

R. PIDDLE or TRENT
WAREHAM
R. FROME
Ridge Wharf

24A

Quay
Lifting Bridge
Hamworthy
FR or G.
19
HBR. OFFICE
CUSTOMS
Coal Q.
Ferry
POOLE Y.C.
Dns.
Fl.5 sec.
13
13
2
1
Yacht Mrgs.
1
2 FR.
6
R.W.
12
13
Fl.5 sec.
1000 FT.

0   CABLES   10

SOUNDINGS IN FEET

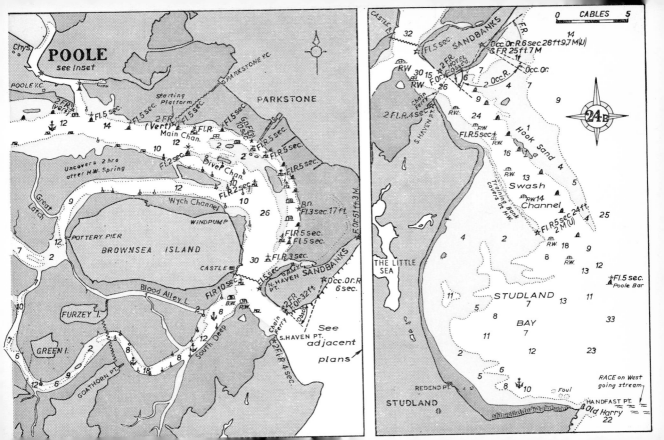

POOLE
see inset

PARKSTONE

2 FR (Vert)
Fl.5 sec.
Fl.5 sec.

PARKSTONE YC

Starting Platform

2 FR (Vert)
Fl.5 sec.
Main Chan.
Fl.R.

Fl.5 sec.
6p FR
2 FR(B)
Fl.5 sec.

POOLE Y.C.
2 FR (Vert)

Chys

Diver Chan.
Fl.R.5 sec.
Fl.R.5 sec.

Uncovers 2 hrs after H.W. Spring

Fl.2 sec.

Wych Channel
Fl.R.2 sec.

Fl.R.5 sec.

Bn. Fl.3 sec.17ft.
F.Or.5ft.3 M

Great Lake

WINDPUMP
26

Fl.5 sec.
Fl.5 sec.

POTTERY PIER
BROWNSEA ISLAND

CASTLE
Fl.5 sec.
Fl.R.3 sec.

30
N.HAVEN SANDBANKS
Occ.Or.R 6 sec.

Blood Alley L.
Fl.R.10 sec.
N.HAVEN PT.
2 FR F.Occ.32ft.
B.W.
R.W.

FURZEY I.

8
South Deep

GREEN I.

GOATHORN PT.
18
2 FL.R.4 sec.

Chain Ferry
S.HAVEN PT.

See adjacent plans

(Chart 24B)

0 — CABLES — 5

32
Fl.5 sec.
SANDBANKS
Occ.Or.R.6 sec.28ft 9.7M(U)
& FR 25 ft.7M

RW
30 15
2 FR HOTEL F.Occ.(3)
Occ.R.
Occ.Or.

RW
26
24B

Chain Ferry
2 Fl.R.4 sec.
S.HAVEN PT.
RW
24
9
1

Hook sand

Fl.R.5 sec.
RW
16

RW

13
Swash
Channel

RW14
Covers at H.W.
Training Bank

Fl.R.5 sec.24ft.
2 M(U)

THE LITTLE SEA

RW. 18
8
RW.
9
13
12

Fl.5 sec.
Poole Bar

STUDLAND
7
13
11

5
BAY
8
7
33

11

2
12
23

5
6

REDEND PT.
10
Foul

RACE on West going stream

HANDFAST PT.
Old Harry
22

STUDLAND

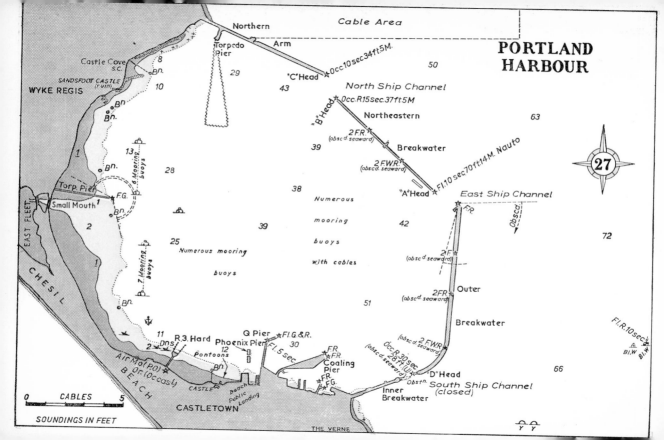

PORTLAND HARBOUR

Cable Area

Northern
Arm

Torpedo
Pier

'C'Head — Occ.10 sec.34 ft.5M.

50

Castle Cove S.C.

SANDSFOOT CASTLE (ruin)

WYKE REGIS

8
Bn.
Bn.
10

29

43

North Ship Channel

'B'Head — Occ.R.15 sec.37 ft.5M

Northeastern

63

Bn.
Bn.

2 F.R. (obsc.d seaward)

Breakwater

13
6 Mooring buoys
Bn.

28

39

39

2 F.W.R. (obsc.d seaward)

Torp.Pier
F.G.
Small Mouth

EAST FLEET

1

38

'A'Head — Fl.10 sec.70 ft.14M. Nauto

East Ship Channel

F.R.

Obsc.d

CHESIL

2

25

Numerous mooring buoys

Numerous

mooring

buoys

with cables

42

72

1

7 Mooring buoys

Bn.

39

51

2 F. (obsc.d seaward)

Outer

2 F.R. (obsc.d seaward)

Breakwater

(obsc.d seaward)

2 F.W.R. (obsc.d seaward)

Fl.R.10 sec.

Bl.W Bl.W

11
R.3.Hard
Dns.
2

Q Pier ★ Fl.G.&R.
Phoenix Pier
Fl.5 sec.

30

F.R.
F.R.

Occ.R.30 sec.
28 ft.(U)

Coaling
Pier

F.R.
F.G.

66

'D'Head
South Ship Channel
(closed)

Air Mol.(Oc.) Or.(Occas.ly)

BEACH

Pontoons

12

Bn.

CASTLE

Beach
Public
Landing

CASTLETOWN

obst.n

Inner
Breakwater

THE VERNE

Y Y

0   CABLES   5

SOUNDINGS IN FEET

27

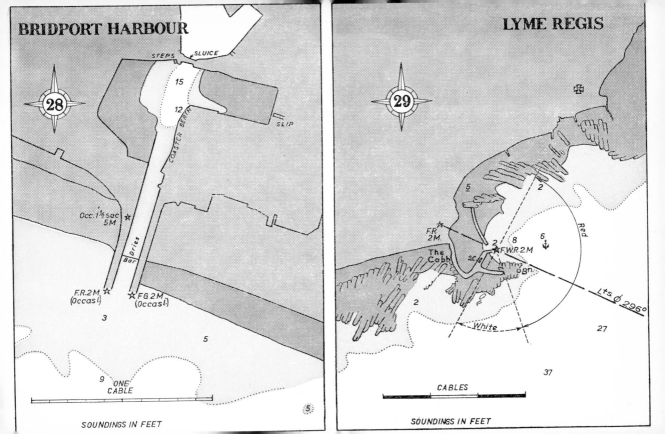

BRIDPORT HARBOUR

28

STEPS · SLUICE

15

12

SLIP

COASTER BERTH

Occ.1½ sec 5M

Dries

Bar

F.R.2M
(Occasl.)

FG 2M
(Occasl.)

3

5

9   ONE
CABLE

SOUNDINGS IN FEET

⑤

LYME REGIS

29

5

2

5

2

F.R.
2M.

The
Cobb

2

8

6

Red

F.WR.2M

Sc.

Bn.

Lts ∅ 296°

White

27

37

CABLES

SOUNDINGS IN FEET

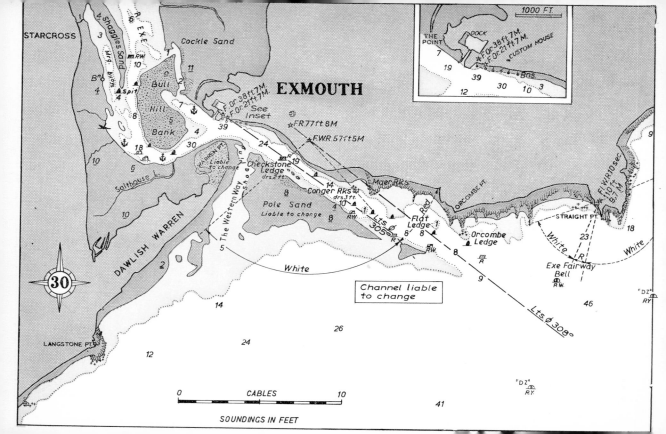

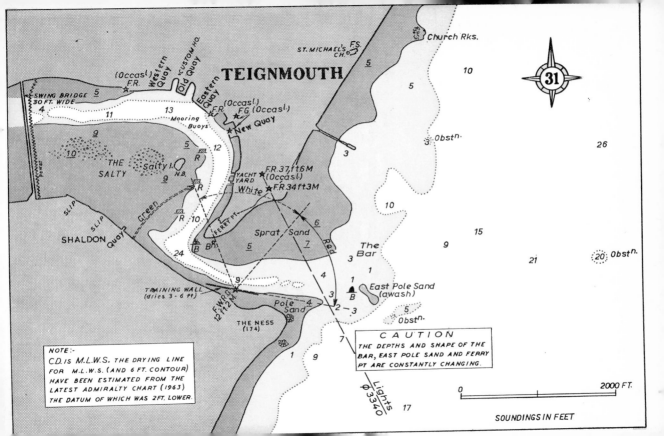

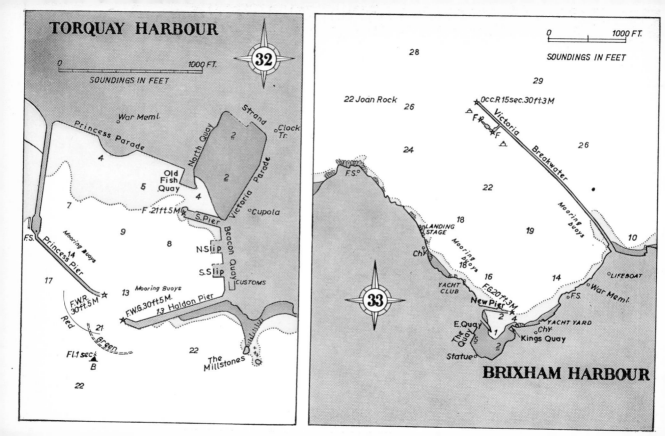

TORQUAY HARBOUR

0   1000 FT.

SOUNDINGS IN FEET

32

War Meml.

Strand

Clock Tr.

Princess Parade

North Quay

4

2

Old Fish Quay

2

5

Victoria Parade

4

Cupola

7

F. 21ft.5M.

S. Pier

9

Beacon Quay

8

N. Slip

S. Slip

CUSTOMS

F.S.

Mooring buoys

Princess Pier

14

17

13   Mooring Buoys

F.W.R. 30ft.5M.

F.W.G. 30ft.5M.

13 Haldon Pier

Red

21

Green

22

The Millstones

Fl.1 sec.

B

22

BRIXHAM HARBOUR

0   1000 FT.

SOUNDINGS IN FEET

28

29

22 Joan Rock   26

Occ.R.15sec.30ft.3M

F. F.

Victoria

24

Breakwater

26

F.S.

22

Mooring buoys

18

LANDING STAGE

19

10

ChY

Mooring buoys

18

YACHT CLUB

16

14

LIFEBOAT

F.G.20ft.3M.

New Pier

War Meml.

2   4

F.S.

E. Quay

1

YACHT YARD

The Quay

5

2

ChY

Kings Quay

Statue

33

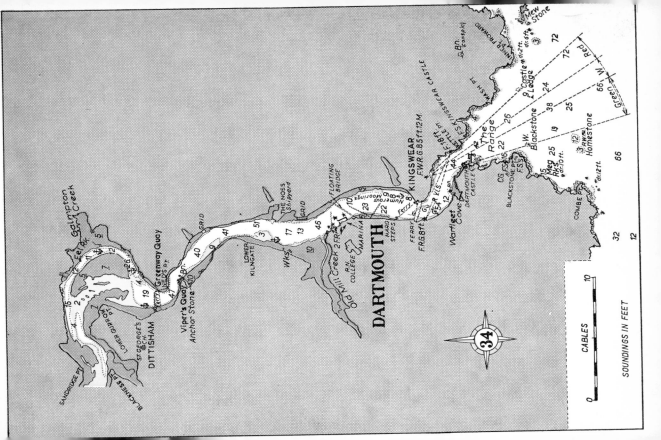

34

CABLES

SOUNDINGS IN FEET

DARTMOUTH

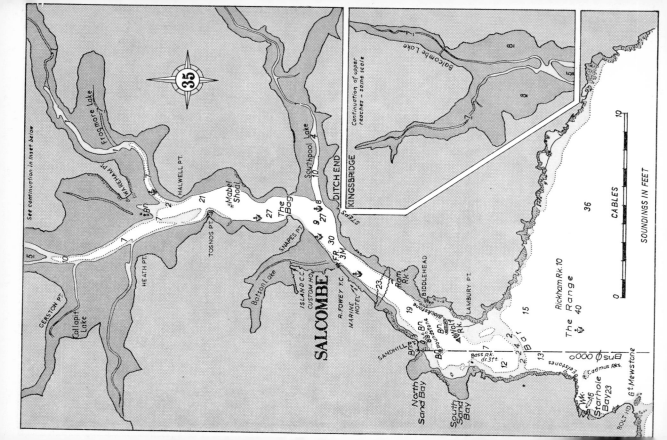

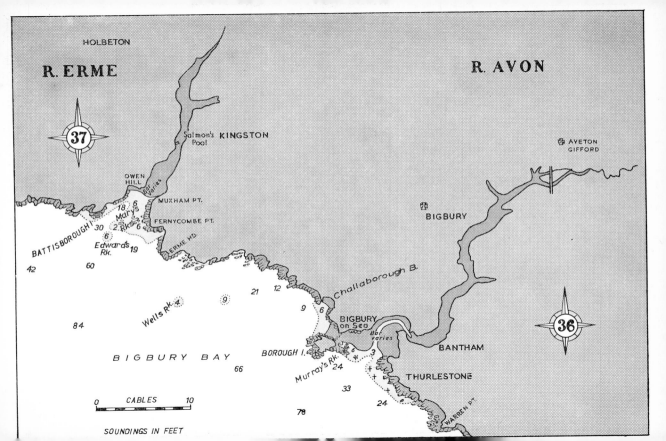

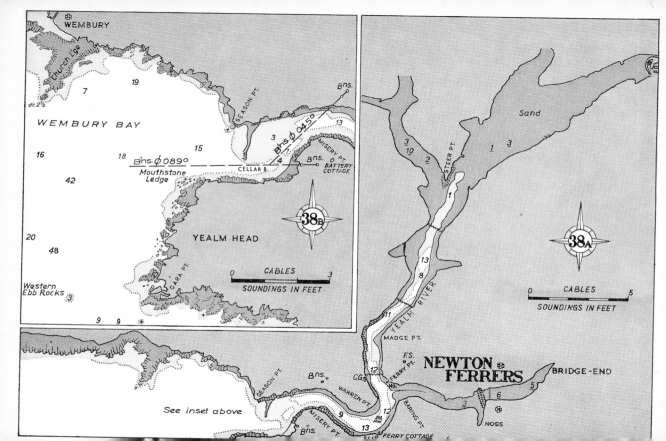

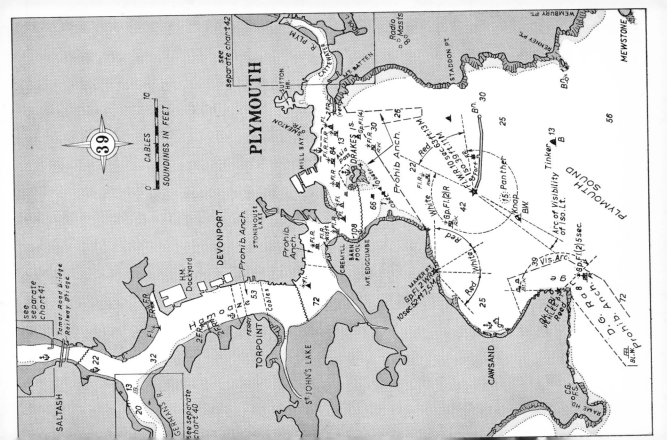

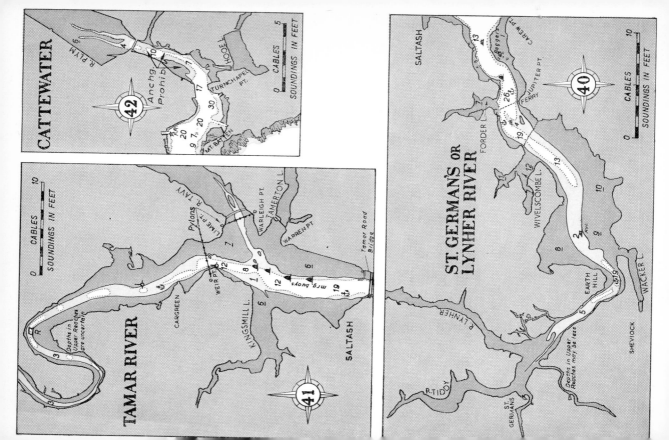

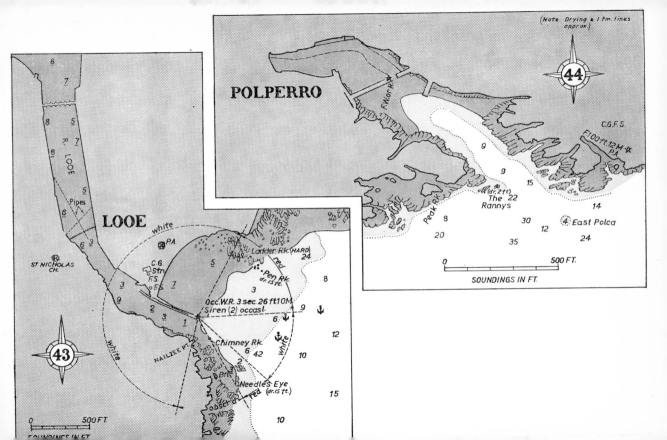

POLPERRO

44

(Note. Drying & 1 fm. lines approx.)

C.G.F.S.

Fl.100 ft.12 M P.A.

F.W.or R.Rk.

9

9

15

Peak Rk.

8

(dr. 2 ft.)
The 22
Rannys

20

30

12

East Polca

14

35

24

0   500 FT.

SOUNDINGS IN FT.

LOOE

R. LOOE

8

7

8   5

7

8   5

5

6

6   3

ST NICHOLAS
CH.

43

white

P.A.

C.G.
Stn.
F.S.
F.S.

Pipes

3

9

2   3   3

1

NAILZEE PT.

white

Chimney Rk.
6 4.2

2

Brn.

observ'd

red

Ladder Rk. (HARD)

5

Pen Rk.
dr. 15 ft.

3

Occ.W.R. 3 sec. 26 ft. 10 M
Siren (2) occasl.

white

Needles Eye
(dr. 15 ft.)

24

8

9

6

12

10

15

10

0   500 FT.

SOUNDINGS IN FT.

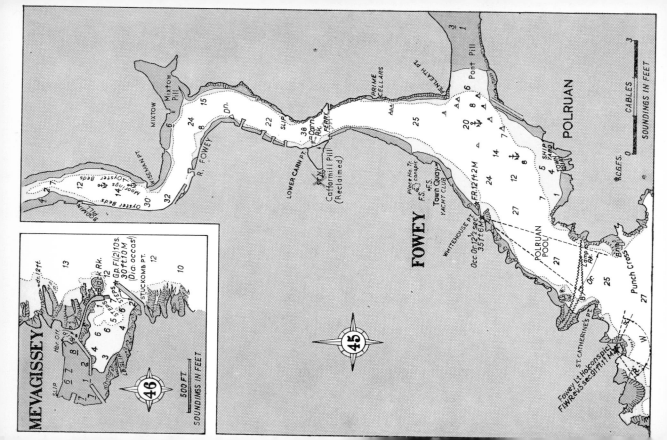

MEVAGISSEY

Hbr. Dir.
Gr. Dir. 12 ft.
13
Br. RK.
STEPS
STEPS 12
S. STEPS Gp.Fl(2)10s.
30 ft.10 M
(Dia: occas.)
STUCKOMB PT.
12
10
SLIP
500 FT
SOUNDINGS IN FEET
46

MIXTOW
Mixtow
Pill
WISEMAN PT.
R. FOWEY
Dir.
Oyster Beds
Moorings
Oyster Beds
BODINNICK
Prime
Cellars
PONLEATH PT.
Pont Pill
LOWER CARN PT.
Carn
Rk.
FERRY
Caffarmill Pill
(Reclaimed)

FOWEY

Place Ho. Tr.
F.S. conspic.
F.S.
Town Quay
YACHT CLUB
FR.12f.2M
WHITEHOUSE PT.
Occ.Or.12½ sec.
35f.6M
Dir.

POLRUAN

SHIP YARD
TOWN QUAY

POLRUAN
POOL
Camp.
Rk.
Dir.
Punch Cross
ST. CATHERINE'S PT.
Fowey Lt.Ho.conspic.
Fl.W.R.&V.S.sec.91f.11f.M.
R.C.G.S.

CABLES
SOUNDINGS IN FEET
45

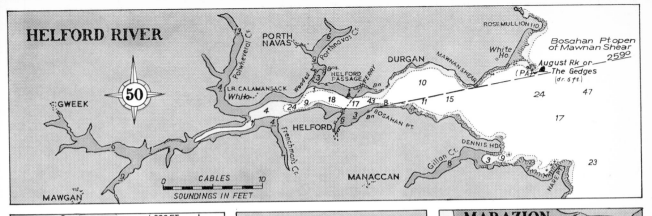

HELFORD RIVER

50

GWEEK

MAWGAN

Polwheveral Cr.

PORTH NAVAS

Porthnavas Cr.

LR. CALAMANSACK
Wh.Ho.

Wooded

Gns.
HELFORD PASSAGE

FERRY

DURGAN

MAWNAN SHEAR

ROSEMULLION HD.

White Ho.

Bosahan Pt.open of Mawnan Shear ___ 259°

August Rk. or The Gedges (dr. 5 ft.)

Frenchman's Cr.

HELFORD

Bn.

Bn.

BOSAHAN PT.

MANACCAN

Gillan Cr.

DENNIS HD.

NARE PT.

13   6   9   6   9   24   18   17   4   9   8   11   15   24   47   17   10   23   3   9   8   7   4   5   4   4   1   2   6   9

CABLES
0 _____ 10
SOUNDINGS IN FEET

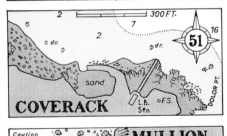

COVERACK

51

300 FT.

sand

dr.   dr.   dr.
L.B. Stn.   o F.S.
DOLOR PT.

2   7   16   2   o   o

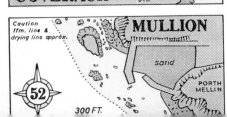

MULLION

52

Caution
1fm. line & drying line approx.

sand

PORTH MELLIN

300 FT.

PORTH LEVEN

53

Inner Hbr.

B.Ho.

F.R. 33 ft 6 M (occ as l)

shingle

500 FT.

6   5   3   1   8   12   6   4   10

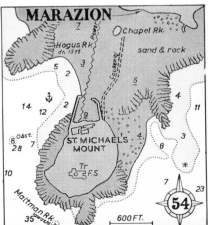

MARAZION

54

Hogus Rk. dr. 15 ft.

Chapel Rk.

sand & rock

Causeway

Power

ST. MICHAEL'S MOUNT

Tr.   o   o F.S.

Maltman Rk. (dries)

Obst.

7   5   3   2   5   4   11   5   2   9   4   3   1   8   14   12   8   28   7   10   35   7   23   Tr.

600 FT.

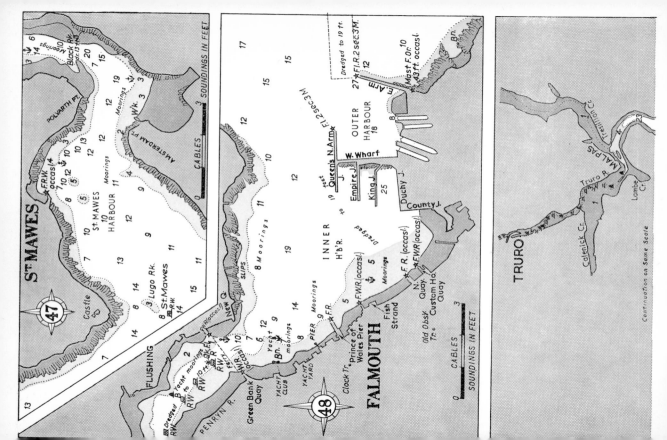

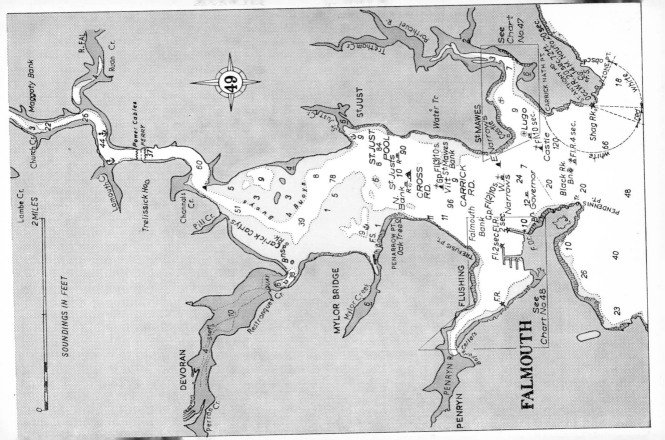

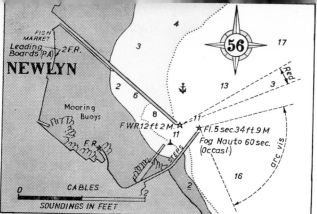

NEWLYN

FISH MARKET
Leading Boards (P.A.) 2 F.R.

Mooring Buoys

F.R.

F W R 12 ft 2 M.

Fl. 5 sec. 34 ft. 9 M
Fog Nauto 60 sec.
(Occas!.)

arc vis.

Red

STEPS

4
3
17
13
3
2
6
8
11
11
2
2
16

CABLES
0   2
SOUNDINGS IN FEET

56

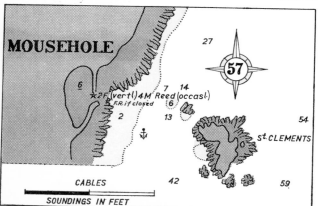

MOUSEHOLE

Mooring

6

★ 2 F (vert!) 4 M Reed (occas!.)
F.R. if closed

2

13
6
7
14

27

54

St CLEMENTS

42   59

CABLES
SOUNDINGS IN FEET

57

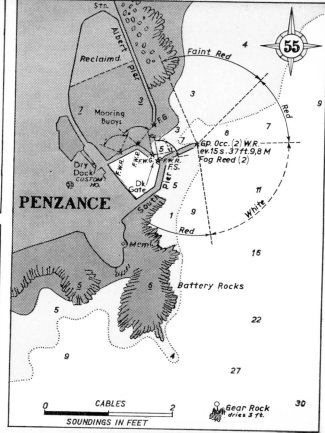

PENZANCE

Stn.
Albert Pier
Reclaim d.
Faint Red

Mooring Buoys

F.G.

Dry Dock
CUSTOM HO.
Dk Gate

F.W.R.
F.W.G.
F.W.R.
F.S.

Gp. Occ. (2) W.R.
ev. 15 s. 37 ft. 9,8 M
Fog Reed (2)

South Pier

Mem.l

Battery Rocks

Gear Rock
dries 3 ft.

4
9
3
7
3
3
5
7
8
7
5
5
1
9
16
22
27
30

Faint Red
Red
White
Red

5
5
6
5
9
4

CABLES
0   2
SOUNDINGS IN FEET

55

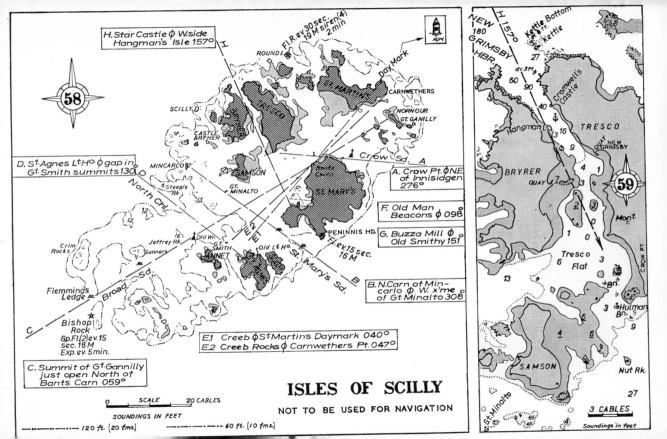

ISLES OF SCILLY

NOT TO BE USED FOR NAVIGATION

58

H. Star Castle φ W.side Hangman's Isle 157°

D. St. Agnes Lt.Ho. φ gap in Gt. Smith summits 130°

A. Crow Pt. φ NE of Innisidgen 276°

F. Old Man Beacons φ 098°

G. Buzza Mill φ Old Smithy 151°

B. N. Carn of Mincarlo φ W. x'me of Gt. Minalto 308°

E1 Creeb φ St. Martins Daymark 040°

E2 Creeb Rocks φ Carnwethers Pt. 047°

C. Summit of Gt. Gannilly just open North of Bants Carn 059°

ROUND I.

Day Mark

Fl.R. ev 30 sec. (4) 19 M siren (4) 2 min

CARNWETHERS

ST. MARY'S

NORNOUR GT. GANILLY

SCILLY O.

CASTLE BRYHER

MINCARLO

GT. MINALTO

Steeple Rk.

Crim Rocks

Jeffrey Rk.

Gunners

GT. SMITH

GANNET

Flemmings Ledge

Broad Sd.

Bishop Rock
Gp.Fl.(2) ev. 15 sec. 18 M
Exp. ev 5 min.

North Chl.

Old Wr.

Old Lt. Ho.

PENINNIS HD.

Fl. ev 15 sec. 16 M

St. Mary's Sd.

Crow Sd.

SCALE 20 CABLES

SOUNDINGS IN FEET

120 ft. (20 fms.)   60 ft. (10 fms.)

59

NEW GRIMSBY HBR.

Kettle Bottom

Kettle

Cromwell's Castle

Hangman I.

TRESCO

NEW GRIMSBY

BRYRER

Mon.t

QUAY

Tresco Flat

Bn.

Hulman Bn.

CROW PT.

SAMSON

Nut Rk.

Gt. Minalto

3 CABLES

Soundings in feet

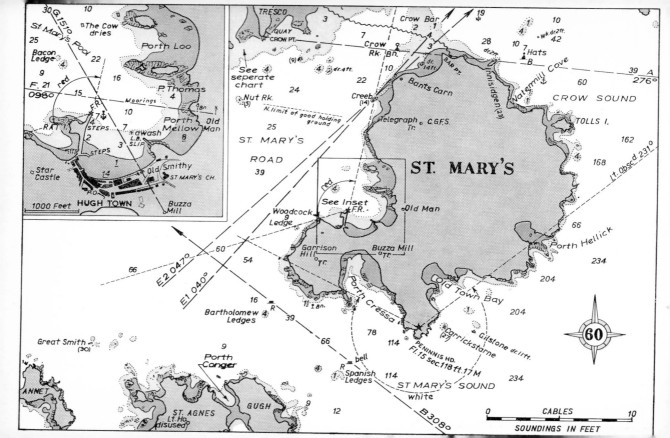

CROW SOUND

ST. MARY'S

ST. MARY'S ROAD

ST. MARY'S SOUND

Inset (top left)
HUGH TOWN

The Cow dries
St. Mary's Pool
Bacon Ledge
F. 21 red
0980
Porth Loo
P. Thomas
Moorings
Old Mellow Man
Porth
awash
L.B. SLIP
STEPS
STEPS
RAT I.
Star Castle
P.O.
Old Smithy
ST. MARY'S CH.
Buzza Mill
1000 Feet

Main chart
TRESCO
Crow Bar
QUAY
CROW PT.
Crow Rk. Bn.
dr. 4ft.
See seperate chart
Nut Rk.
(5)
N. limit of good holding ground
Creeb (14)
Bants Carn
Watermill Cove
Hats
B
Wk. dr. 2ft.
42
Innisidgen (23)
Telegraph Tr.
C.G.F.S.
TOLLS I.
276°
39 A
60
162
168
Lt. obscd 231°
See Inset
red
F.R.
Old Man
66
Porth Hellick
Woodcock Ledge
Garrison Hill
Tr.
Buzza Mill Tr.
Old Town Bay
204
234
E 2 047°
E 1 040°
Porth Cressa
Bartholomew Ledges
R
Great Smith (30)
Porth Conger
Gistone dr. 11ft.
Carrickstarne (27)
PENINNIS HD.
Fl. 15 sec. 118 ft. 17 M
204
234
R bell
Spanish Ledges
ST MARY'S SOUND
white
ANNET
ST. AGNES
Lt. Ho. disused
GUGH
B 3080
12

60

CABLES 0 ————— 10
SOUNDINGS IN FEET

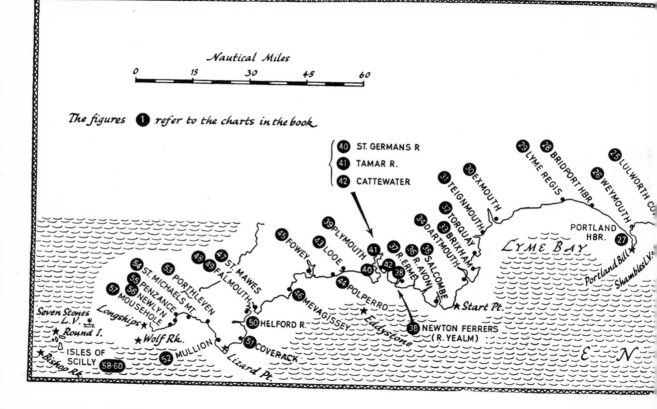